General Gordon Saint And Soldier

by

Joseph Wardle

Double 9 BOOKS

General Gordon Saint And Soldier
by Joseph Wardle

ISBN: 978-93-61426-54-4

Published by

DOUBLE 9 BOOKS
2/13-B, Ansari Road
Daryaganj, New Delhi – 110002
info@double9books.com
www.double9books.com
Tel. 011-40042856

ABOUT THE AUTHOR

Joseph Wardle, an outstanding writer renowned for his insightful biographies and historical narratives, penned an excellent masterpiece titled "General Gordon: Saint and Soldier." Wardle's paintings delves into the captivating existence and profound legacy of General Charles George Gordon, a parent of vast significance in British navy records. In "General Gordon: Saint and Soldier," Wardle meticulously explores the multifaceted persona of Gordon, depicting him no longer only as a pro army chief but also as a man deeply guided via his spiritual convictions and ethical standards. Through meticulous research and vibrant storytelling, Wardle sheds light on Gordon's splendid exploits, from his valiant navy campaigns in various corners of the sector to his unwavering dedication to humanitarian causes and his eventual martyrdom in Khartoum. Wardle's narrative skillfully navigates via Gordon's triumphs and tribulations, imparting readers a complete portrait of a person whose unwavering faith, courage, and selflessness left an indelible mark on history. "General Gordon: Saint and Soldier" stands as a testomony to Wardle's prowess as a biographer and historian, capturing the essence of a terrific individual whose life maintains to inspire generations.

CONTENTS

PREFACE

Nothing but the greatest possible pressure from my many kind friends who have heard my lecture on "General Gordon: Saint and Soldier," who knew of my intimacy with him, and had seen some of the letters referred to, would have induced me to narrate this little story of a noble life. I am greatly indebted to many friends, authors, and newspapers, for extracts and incidents, etc., etc.; and to them I beg to offer my best thanks and humble apology. This book is issued in the hope, that, with all its imperfections, it may inspire the young men of our times to imitate the Christ-like spirit and example of our illustrious and noble hero, C. G. Gordon.

J. Wardle.

THIS BRIEF STORY
OF A
NOBLE, SAINTLY and HEROIC LIFE,
I DEDICATE WITH MUCH AFFECTION
TO MY SON,
JOSEPH GORDON WARDLE

"If I am asked, who is the greatest man? I answer, "the best." And if I am requested to say, who is the best, I reply: "he that deserveth most of his fellow creatures."

—*Sir William Jones.*

CHAPTER I

"There is nothing purer than honesty; nothing sweeter than charity; nothing warmer than love; nothing richer than wisdom; nothing brighter than virtue; nothing more steadfast than faith." —*Bacon.*

It has been said that the most interesting study for mankind is man; and surely one of the grandest objects for human contemplation, is a noble character; a lofty type of a truly great and good man is humanity's richest heritage.

The following lines by one of our greatest poets are true—

"Lives of great men all remind us,
We can make our lives sublime,
And departing leave behind us,
Footprints on the sands of time."

While places and things may have a special or peculiar charm, and indeed may become very interesting, nothing stirs our hearts, or rouses our enthusiasm so much as the study of a noble heroic life, such as that of the uncrowned king, who is the subject of our story, and whose career of unsullied splendour closed in the year 1885 in the beleaguered capital of that dark sad land, where the White and Blue Nile blend their waters.

"Noble he was contemning all things mean,
His truth unquestioned and his soul severe,
At no man's question was he e'er dismayed,
Of no man's presence was he e'er afraid."

General Gordon was the son of a soldier who proved his gallantry on many occasions, and who took a pride in his profession. It was said of him that he was greatly beloved by all who served under him. He was generous, genial and kind hearted, and strictly just in all his practices and aims. He gave to his Queen and country a long life of devoted service. His wife, we are told, was a woman of marked liberality; cheerful and loving, always thoughtful of the wants of others; completely devoid of selfishness.

The fourth son, and third soldier of this happy pair, Charles George, was born at Woolwich in 1833. He was trained at Taunton. When about 15 years of age he was sent to the Royal Military Academy at Woolwich, to prepare for the army; a profession his father thought most worthy of the Gordons. While here at school an incident occurred which served to show that our young hero was no ordinary student. His tutor, with an air of contempt, rebuked him severely for some error or failure in his lessons, and told him sneeringly he would never make a general. This roused the Scotch blood of the budding soldier, and in a rage he tore the epaulettes from his shoulders, and threw them at his tutor's feet—another proof of the correctness of the old adage, "Never prophesy unless you know." By the time he reached the age of twenty-one, he had become every inch a soldier, and when tested he proved to have all a soldier's qualities—bravery, courage, heroism, patriotism, and fidelity, characteristics of the best soldiers in our army.

Archibald Forbes, writing of him, says "The character of General Gordon was unique. As it unfolded in its curiously varied but never contradictory aspects, you are reminded of Cromwell, of Havelock, of Livingstone, and of Captain Hedley Viccars. But Gordon's individuality stood out in its incomparable blending of masterfulness and tenderness, of strength and sweetness. His high and noble nature was made more chivalrous by his fervent, deep and real piety. His absolute trust in God guided him serenely through the greatest difficulties. Because of that he was not alone in the deepest solitude. He was not depressed in the direst extremity. He had learned the happy art of leaning upon the Omnipotent arm."

GORDON, THE HERO.

Early in 1884 a leading newspaper said of him, "General Gordon is without doubt the finest captain of irregular forces living." About the same time Mr. Gladstone said of him, "General Gordon is no common man. It is no exaggeration to say he is a hero. It is no exaggeration to say he is a Christian hero." Mr. W. E. Forster also remarked of him, "I know no other man living for whom I have a greater admiration than General Gordon. He is utterly unselfish. He is regardless of money. He cares nothing for fame or glory. He cares little for life or death. He is a deeply religious man. The world to come, and God's government over this, are to him the greatest of life's realities. True heroism has been said to be a sacrifice of self for the benefit of others. If this is true, Gordon has well won the appellation, "The Hero of the Soudan." His soldierly qualities were first tested in the Crimea, where we find him in 1854 and 1855. Here for the first time in his military career he was brought face to face with all the horrors of actual war, and here for the first time he saw friend and foe lie locked like brothers in each other's arms. Here he got his first baptism of fire; and here he showed the splendid qualities which in after years made him so famous and so beloved. An old soldier who served under him during this terrible campaign says "I shall never forget that remarkable figure and form, which was an inspiration to all who knew him, and saw him on the field of carnage and blood."

He was utterly unconcerned in the midst of dangers and death. He would twirl his cane and good humouredly say "Now boys, don't fear, I see no danger." On one occasion when engaged in the very thick of a most awful struggle he said, "Now my boys, I'm your officer, I lead, you follow," and he walked literally through a shower of lead and iron with as little concern apparently, as if he were walking across his own drawing-room; and he came out of the conflict without a scar.

Sir E. Stanton in his dispatches home, making special reference to our hero, says—"Young Gordon has attracted the notice of his superiors out here, not only by his activity, but by his special aptitude for war, developing itself amid the trenches before Sebastopol, in a personal knowledge of the enemy's movements, such as no officer has displayed. We have sent him frequently right up to the Russian entrenchments to find out what new moves they are making." Amid all the excitement of war and its dangers he never omitted writing to his mother; an example I hope my readers, if boys, or girls, will studiously copy. He loved his mother with the passion of his great loving heart. Soldier lads often forget their mother's influence, their mother's prayers, and their mother's God. Writing home to his mother he says "We are giving the Redan shells day and night, in order to prevent the Russians from repairing it and they repay us by sending amongst us awful missiles of death and destruction, and it requires one to be very nimble to keep out of their way. I have now been thirty-four times, twenty-four hours in the trenches; that is more than a month without any relief whatever, and I assure you it gets very tedious. Still one does not mind if any advance is being made."

An eye witness of this bloody work in the trenches and the storming of the Malakof and the Redan, writes:—

> "On that terrible 8th of September, every gun and mortar that our people and our noble allies, the French, could bring to bear upon the enemy's work, was raining death and destruction upon them. The stormers had all got into their places. They consisted of about 1,000 men of the Old Light and 2nd Division; the supports were formed up as closely as possible to them, and all appeared in readiness. History may well say, 'the storming of a fortress is an awful task.' There we stood not a word being spoken; every one seemed to be full of thought; many a courageous heart, that was destined to be still in death in one short hour, was now beating high."
>
> "It was about 11.15 a.m., and our heavy guns were firing in such a way as I have never heard before. The batteries fired in volleys or salvoes as fast as they could load and fire, the balls passing a few feet above our heads, while the air seemed full of shell. The enemy were not idle; for round shot, shell, grape and musket balls were bounding and whizzing all about us, and earth and stones were rattling about our heads like hail. Our poor fellows fell fast, but still our sailors and artillery men stuck to it manfully. We knew well that this could not last long, but many a brave soldier's career was cut short long before we advanced to the attack—strange some of our older hands were smoking and taking not the slightest notice of this 'dance of death.' Some men were being carried past dead, and others limping to the rear

with mangled limbs, while their life's blood was streaming fast away. We looked at each other with amazement for we were now under a most terrible fire. We knew well it meant death to many of us. Several who had gone through the whole campaign shook hands saying, 'This is hot,' 'Good bye, old boy,' 'Write to the old folks for me if I do not return.' This request was made by many of us. I was close to one of our Generals, who stood watch in hand, when suddenly at 12 o'clock mid-day the French drums and bugles sounded the charge, and with a shout, 'Vive l'Empereur' repeated over and over again by some 50,000 men, a shout that was enough to strike terror into the enemy. The French, headed by the Zouaves, sprang forward at the Malakof like a lot of cats. On they went like a lot of bees, or rather like the dashing of the waves of the sea against a rock. We had a splendid view of their operations, it was grand but terrible; the deafening shouts of the advancing hosts told us they were carrying all before them."

"They were now completely enveloped in smoke and fire, but column after column kept advancing, pouring volley after volley into the breasts of the defenders. They (the French) meant to have it, let the cost be what it might. At 12.15 up went the proud flag of France, with a shout that drowned for a time the roar of both cannon and musketry. And now came our turn. As soon as the French were seen upon the Malakof our stormers sprang forward, led by Colonel Windham—the old Light Division consisting of 300 men of the 90th, about the same number of the 97th, and about 400 of the 2nd Battalion Rifle Brigade, and with various detachments of the 2nd and Light Divisions, and a number of blue jackets, carrying scaling ladders. Our men advanced splendidly, with a ringing British cheer, although the enemy poured a terrible fire of grape, canister and musketry into them, which swept down whole companies at a time. We, the supports, moved forward to back up our comrades. We advanced as quickly as we could until we came to the foremost trench, when we leaped the parapet, then made a rush at the blood stained walls of the Redan. We had had a clear run of over 200 yards under that murderous fire of grape, canister and musketry. How any ever lived to pass that 200 yards seemed a miracle; for our poor fellows fell one on the top of another; but nothing could stop us but death. On we went shouting until we reached the redoubt. The fighting inside these works was of the most desperate character, butt and bayonet, foot and fist; the enemy's guns were quickly spiked: this struggle lasted about an hour and a half. It was an awful time, about 3,000 of our brave soldiers were slain in this short period." Our hero Gordon, tells us that on the evening of this 8th of September—

"I heard most terrific explosions, the earth seemed to be shaken to its very centre;—It was afterwards discovered the enemy's position was no longer tenable, so they had fired some 300 tons of gunpowder, which had blown up all their vast forts and magazines. O! what a night: many of our poor fellows had been nearly buried in the *debris*, and burning mass: the whole of Sebastopol was in flames. The Russians were leaving it helter-skelter—a complete rout, and a heavy but gloriously-won victory."

For his acknowledged ability, his fine heroism, and his true loyalty to his superiors during this most trying campaign, he received the well-earned decoration of the Legion of Honour from the French Government, a mark of distinction very rarely conferred upon so young an officer.

"God gives us men, a time like that demands.
Strong minds, great hearts, true faith and ready hands;
Men whom the lusts of office cannot kill,
Men whom the spoils of office cannot buy,
Men who possess opinions and a will,
Men who have honour, men who never lie."

We must not leave this part of our story without a brief notice of one whose name will live in song and story, when this generation shall have passed away. Many noble English ladies bravely went out to nurse the suffering soldiers; but in this noble band was one whose name remains a synonym for kindly sympathy, tenderness and peace—Miss Florence Nightingale.

The following lines were written in her praise—

"Britain has welcomed home with open hand
Her gallant soldiers to their native land;
But one alone the Nation's thanks did shun,
Though Europe rings with all that she hath done;
For when will shadow on the wall e'er fail,
To picture forth fair Florence Nightingale:
Her deeds are blazoned on the scroll of fame,
And England well may prize her deathless name."

CHAPTER II

"The greatness of a nation depends upon the men it can breed and rear.—*Froude.*

The war over and peace duly established, Lieutenant Gordon (for so he was then) accompanied General Sir Lintorn Simmons to Galatz, where, as assistant commissioner, he was engaged in fixing the new frontiers of Russia, Turkey and Roumania. In 1857, when his duties here were finished, he went with the same officer to Armenia; there, in the same capacity, he was engaged in laying down the Asiatic frontiers of Russia and Turkey. When this work was completed he returned home and was quartered at Chatham, and employed for a time as Field Work Instructor and Adjutant. In 1860, now holding the rank of Captain, he joined the Army in China, and was present at the surrender of Pekin; and for his services he was promoted to the rank of Major.

THE BURNING OF THE SUMMER PALACE

"On the eleventh of October," Gordon relates, "we were sent down in a hurry to throw up earth works against the City; as the Chinese refused to give up the gate we demanded their surrender before we could treat with them. They were also required to give up the prisoners. You will be sorry to hear the treatment they have suffered has been very bad. Poor De Norman, who was with me in Asia, is one of the victims. It appears they were tied so tight by the wrists that the flesh mortified, and they died in the greatest torture. Up to the time that elapsed before they arrived at the Summer Palace, they were well treated, but then the ill-treatment began. The Emperor is supposed to have been there at the time.

But to go back to the work, the Chinese were given until twelve on the 13th, to give up the gate. We made a lot of batteries, and everything was ready for assault of the wall, which is a battlement, forty feet high, but of inferior masonry; at 11.30 p.m., however, the gate was opened, and we took possession; so our work was of no avail. The Chinese had then, until the 23rd, to think over our terms of treaty, and to pay up ten thousand pounds (£10,000) for each Englishman, and five hundred pounds (£500) for each native soldier who had died during their captivity. This they did, and the money was paid, and the treaty signed yesterday. I could not witness it, as all officers commanding companies were obliged to remain in camp, owing to the ill-treatment the prisoners experienced at the Summer Palace. The General ordered this to be destroyed, and stuck up proclamations to say why it was ordered. We accordingly went out, and after pillaging it, burned the whole magnificent palace, and destroyed most valuable property, which could not be replaced for millions of pounds.

"This Palace" (wrote the author of *Our Own Times*), "covered an area of many miles. The Palace of Adrian, at Tivoli, might have been hidden in one of its courts. Gardens, temples, small lodges and pagodas, groves, grottoes, lakes, bridges, terraces, artificial hills, diversified the vast space. All the artistic treasures, all the curiosities, archæological and other, that Chinese wealth and taste, such as it was, could bring together." Gordon notes, "This palace, with its surrounding buildings, over two hundred in number, covered an area eight by ten miles in extent." He says, "it makes one's heart burn to see such beauty destroyed; it was as if Windsor Palace, South Kensington Museum, and British Museum, all in one, were in flames: you can scarcely imagine the beauty and magnificence of the things we were bound to destroy."

"These palaces were so large, and we were so pressed for time, that we could not plunder them carefully. Quantities of gold ornaments were burned, considered as brass. It was wretchedly demoralizing for an army: everybody was wild for plunder . . . The throne and room were lined with ebony, carved in a wonderful manner. There were huge mirrors of all shapes and sizes, clocks, watches, musical boxes with puppets on them, magnificent china of every description, heaps and heaps of silks of all colours, coral screens, large amounts of treasures, etc. The French have smashed up everything in a most shameful way. It was a scene of utter destruction which passes my description." This was not much in Gordon's line.

In the following year he made a tour on horseback to the outer wall of China at Kalgan, accompanied by Lieutenant Cardew. A Chinese lad of the age of fourteen, who knew a little English, acted as their servant and interpreter, while their personal luggage was conveyed in the Chinese carts. In the course of this tour we are told they passed through districts which had never before been visited by any European. At Kalgan the great wall was seen, with its parapet about twenty-two feet high, and sixteen feet broad. Both sides were solid brick, each being three times the size of our English bricks. Gordon writes: "It is wonderful to see the long line of wall stretching over the hills as far as the eye can reach." From Kalgan they travelled westwards to Taitong; here they saw huge caravans of camels laden with tea going towards Russia. Here they were forced to have the axle trees of their carts widened, for they had come into a great part of the country where the wheels were set wider than in the provinces whence they came. Their carts, therefore, no longer fitted into the deep ruts which had been worn into the terribly bad roads. The main object of their journey was to find out if there was in the Inner Wall any pass besides the Tchatiaou which on that side of the country led from the Russian territory to Pekin. It was not until they reached Taiyuen that they struck the road that led to Pekin or Tientsin.

Their first bit of trouble on this somewhat venturesome tour occurred at Taiyneu; when the bill was brought for their night's entertainment, they found it was most exorbitant. They saw they were likely to have trouble, so they sent on the carts with luggage and waited at this strange hostelry till they believed they had got well out of the way. Then they offered what they believed was a reasonable amount in payment of their bill. It was refused. They then tried to mount their horses but the people at the Inn stopped them. Major Gordon hereupon drew his revolver more for show than for use, for he allowed them to take it from him. He then said, "Let us go to the Mandarin's house." To this consent was given, and the two wide-awake English officers walked alongside their horses. On the way Gordon said to his companion "are you ready to mount?" "Yes" he replied. So they mounted quietly, and went on with the people. When they reached the Mandarin's, they turned their horses and galloped off after their carts as fast as they could, having paid what they believed a reasonable amount for expenses. The people yelled and rushed after them, but it was too late. Some distance from the place where they had spent the night they came upon the pass over the mountains which led down into the country, drained by the great Peiho river. "The descent" says Gordon, "was terrible, and the cold so intense that raw eggs were frozen as hard as if they had been boiled half an hour." To add to their troubles, the carts they had sent on in front had been attacked by robbers. They, however, with many difficulties managed to reach Tientsin in safety; their leave of absence had been exceeded by about fourteen days. In 1862 Major Gordon left for Shanghai under the orders of Sir Charles Staveley who had been appointed to the command of the English forces in China. At the very time that England and France were at war with China, a terrible and far reaching rebellion was laying waste whole provinces. An article in our London *Daily News* about this date said, "But for Gordon the whole Continent of China might have been a scene of utter and hopeless ruin and devastation." At the date he took charge of the "ever victorious army," China was in a state of widespread anarchy and confusion.

This rebellion which Gordon was here authorized to suppress was called "The Tai-ping rebellion." Its rise was brought about by a strange mixture of incredulity and fanaticism, caused by some European Christian giving away his literature. A village demagogue named Hung-tsne-Shuen caught the idea, after reading the papers referred to, that he was inspired; that he was God, King, Emperor, and that he ought to rule; so, puffed up with pride and insatiable ambition, he began raising an army; and aimed at nothing less than the usurpation of the "Dragon Throne." Some thought him mad; but he gathered about him some 20,000 men whom he had influenced to believe in him as the "Second Celestial Brother," and gave out he was a seer of visions, a prophet of vengeance and freedom; a champion of the poor and oppressed; and many were mad enough to believe him, and thus he raised an army which grew in strength until it reached some hundreds of thousands strong; he then proclaimed himself the Heavenly King, The Emperor of the great place; and then with five wangs or warrior kings, chosen from amongst his kinsmen, he marched through China, devastating the country, and increasing his army in his progress.

The most populous, and until now wealthy provinces were soon in his hands. The silk factories were silent; the Cities were falling into utter and hopeless desolation: rebellion, war and famine, raged and reigned supreme. Gordon made them pause! His marvellous power of organizing and leading men, a power derived from an inflexible, determined, fearless, and deeply religious temperament, influenced the Chinese character quickly and powerfully. His very name soon became a terror to the banded brigands and to all evil doers. An Englishman in China at the time wrote home and said "The destiny of China is in the hands of Major Gordon, and if he remains at his post the question will soon be settled, and peace and quiet will be restored to this unfortunate, but sorely tried country."

In all the strange and trying experiences of this Chinese Campaign Gordon bore himself with a bravery and courage seldom equalled, we think never surpassed.

Dr. Guthrie once said, "It is very remarkable, and highly creditable to the loyalty and bravery of our British soldiers, that, notwithstanding all the wars in which they have been engaged, no foreign nation to-day flaunts a British flag as a trophy of its victory and of our defeat. Nor in the proud pillar raised by the great Napoleon in commemoration of his many victories—a pillar made of the cannons taken by him in battles, is there an ounce of metal that belongs to a British gun." The characteristics of the bravest of our British soldiers were pre-eminently displayed in Gordon. For—

"He holds no party with unmanly fears,
Where duty points he confidently steers:
Faces a thousand dangers at her call,
And trusting in his God surmounts them all."

His soldierly qualities were very often put to the test in this strange land. Hung, the leader of this rebellion, had become so popular and made such marvellous progress that when Gordon had organized his ever victorious army, Hung had captured Nanking, one of the principal cities, and made this his capital; and here, under the very shadow of the Chinese metropolis, he established himself in royal state. His followers were held together by the force of his religious tenets; they believed in him as the Lord from Heaven, who would save the suffering minds and give them a celestial reward. A missionary who was in Nanking, Rev. J. L. Holmes, gives his impressions of this warlike devotee. "At night (he says) we witnessed their worship. It occurred at the beginning of their sabbath, midnight on Friday. The place of worship was the Chung-Wang's private audience room. He was himself seated in the midst of his attendants, no females were present. They first sang, or rather chanted; after which a written prayer was read, then burned by an officer; then they rose and sang again, then separated. The Chung-wang sent for me before he left his seat, and asked me if I understood their mode of worship. I replied I had just seen it for the first time. He explained that the Tien-wang had been to the celestial world and had seen the Great God and obtained a revelation! &c. . . . As the day dawned we started for the Palace of the Tien-wang. The procession was headed by a number of brilliantly coloured banners, after which followed a troop of armed soldiers; then came the Chung-wang in a large sedan, covered with yellow satin and embroidery, and borne by eight coolies. Music of a peculiar kind added to the scene, as the curious sightseers lined the streets on either side, who probably never saw such a sight before. Reaching the "Morning Palace," we were presented to the Tsau-wang and his son with several others including the Tien-wang's two brothers, who were seated in a deep recess over the entrance of which was written "Illustrious Heavenly Door." In another place was "Holy Heavenly Gate," from which a boy of about fourteen made his appearance and took his place with the royal group; then they proceeded with their religious ceremonies again: this time kneeling with their faces to the Tien-wang's seat. Then they sang in a standing position. A roast pig and the body of a goat were lying with other articles on tables in the outer court, and a fire was kept burning on a stone altar in the front of the Tien-wang's seat. Afterwards, says the missionary, I was led through a number of rooms and courts to see Chung-wang privately. I was brought into one of his private sitting-rooms, where he sat clothed loosely in white silk, with a red kerchief round his head, and a jewel in front. He was seated in an easy chair, and fanned by a pretty slipshod girl. He asked me to a seat beside him and questioned me about a map he had seen with parallel lines running each way, said to have been made by foreigners, asked me to explain what it was. He also showed me a musical-box and a spy-glass, asking many questions. From all I could learn by my visit to this pretender there was nothing in their religion to elevate, but everything to degrade. With them to rob and murder were virtuous deeds. "Slay the imps" was their watchword. Gordon found in this fanatic a foe of no mean order. But he soon found too that courage and faith in God had done and would still lead to victory. In a letter home he says—"I am afraid you will be much vexed at my having taken the command of the Sung-kiang force, and that I am now a mandarin. I have taken the step on consideration. I think that any one who contributes to putting down this rebellion fulfils a human task, and also tends a great deal to open China to civilization. I will not act rashly, and I trust to be able soon to return to England; at the same time I will remember your and my father's wishes, and endeavour to remain as short a time as possible. I can say that if I had not accepted the command I believe the force would have been broken up and the rebellion gone on in its misery for years. I trust this will not now be the case, and that I may soon be able to comfort you on this subject. You must not fret about me, I think I am doing a good service . . . I keep your likeness before me, and can assure you and my father that I will not be rash, and that as soon as I can conveniently, and with due regard to the object I have in view, I will come home."

Gordon had hardly yet realized the difficulties and dangers which beset him. His troops were undisciplined and largely composed of all nationalities. Men bent on plunder, and exceedingly numerous; about 120,000 men. Gordon's appointment as Chief in Command of the "Ever Victorious Army" proved to be a wise and good one for China.

Colonel Chesney thus writes:—"If General Staveley had made a mistake in the operations he personally conducted the year before, he more than redeemed it by the excellence of his choice of Gordon. This strange army was made up of French, Germans, Americans, Spaniards, some of good and some of bad character, but in their chief they had one whose courage they were bound to admire, and whose justice they could not help but admit. The private plundering of vanquished towns and cities allowed under their former chief, disappeared under the eye of a leader whose eye was as keen, as his soul was free from the love of filthy lucre. They, however, learned to respect and love a general in whose kindness, valour, skill, and justice they found cause unhesitatingly to confide; who never spared himself personal exposure when danger was near. In every engagement, and these numbered more than seventy, he was to the front and led in person. His somewhat undisciplined army, had in it many brave men; but even such men were very reluctant at times to face these desperate odds. Whenever they showed signs of vacillation he would take one of the men by the arm, and lead him into the very thick of the fight. He always went unarmed even when foremost in the breach. He never saw danger. A shower of bullets was no more to him than a shower of hailstones; he carried one weapon only, and that was a little cane, which won for itself the name of "Gordon's magic wand." On one occasion when leading a storming party his men wavered under a most withering fire. Gordon coolly turned round and waving his cane, bade his men follow him. The soldiers inspired by his courage, followed with a tremendous rush and shout, and at once grandly carried the position. After the capture of one of the Cities, Gordon was firm in not allowing them to pillage, sack and burn such places; and for this some of his men showed a spirit of insubordination. His artillery men refused to fall in when ordered; nay more, they threatened to turn upon him their guns and blow him and his officers to pieces. This news was conveyed to him by a written declaration. His keen eye saw through their scheme at a glance, and with that quiet determination which was his peculiar strength, he summoned them into his presence and with a firmness born of courage and faith in God, he declared that unless the ringleader of this movement was given up, one out of every five would be shot! At the same time he stepped to the front and with his own hand seized one of the most suspicious looking of the men, dragged him out, and ordered him to be shot on the spot at once, the order was instantly carried out by an officer. After this he gave them half an hour to reconsider their position at the end of which he found them ready to carry out any order he might give. It transpired afterwards that the man who was shot was the ringleader in this insubordination."

When Gordon had broken the neck of this far-reaching and disastrous rebellion, and had restored to the Emperor of China the principal cities and towns in peace, the London *Times* wrote of him:—"Never did a soldier of fortune deport himself with a nicer sense of military honour, with more gallantry against the resisting, with more mercy towards the vanquished, with more disinterested neglect of opportunities of personal advantage, or with more entire devotion to the objects and desires of the Government he served, than this officer, who, after all his splendid victories, has just laid down his sword."

Before leaving China he was offered a very large reward in cash, as it was acknowledged on all hands he had saved the Empire more than £5,000,000 sterling. All money he refused; he, however, asked that some of it might be given to the troops, who had served him on the whole with great loyalty, and this was granted. A gold medal was struck in honour of his marvellous achievements, and this he accepted and brought home; but it was soon missing. He thought more of the starving poor than of any medal; so he sold it, and sent the cash it realized to the Lancashire Cotton Operatives, who were then literally starving. The Imperial Decree of China conferred upon him the rank of "Ti-tu," the very highest honour ever conferred upon a Chinese subject. Also the "Peacock's feather," "The Order of the Star," and the "Yellow Jacket." By these he was constituted one of the "Emperor's Body Guard." In a letter home he says, "I shall leave China as poor as I entered it, but with the knowledge that through my weak instrumentality from eighty to one hundred thousand lives have been saved. Than this I covet no greater satisfaction."

Before he left China, as a proof of the estimation in which he was held, a grand illuminated address was presented to him, signed by more than sixty of the leading firms of the Empire, and by most of the bankers and merchants of the cities of Pekin, Shanghai, and of the principal towns throughout China.

It read thus:—"Honoured Sir,—On the eve of your departure to your native country, we, the undersigned, mostly fellow-countrymen of your own, but also representing other nationalities, desire to express to you our earnest wish for a successful voyage and happy return to your friends and the land of your birth.

"Your career during your stay amongst us has been, so far as we know, without a parallel in the history of foreign nations with China; and we feel that we should be alike wanting towards you and towards ourselves, were we to pass by this opportunity without expressing our appreciation and admiration of the line of conduct which you personally have pursued. In a position of unequalled difficulty, and surrounded by complications of every conceivable nature, you have succeeded in offering to the eyes of the Chinese Empire, no less by your loyal and thoroughly disinterested line of action than by your conspicuous gallantry and talent for organization and command, the example of a foreign officer, serving the government of this country, with honourable fidelity and undeviating self-respect.

CHINESE GORDON.

"Once more wishing you a prosperous voyage, and a long career of usefulness and success."

Signed, &c.

There is truth in this as applied to Gordon:—

"He strove not for the wealth of fame,
From heaven the power that moved him came.
And welcome as the mountain air,
The voice that bid him do and dare.
Onward he bore and battled still
With a most firm enduring will,
His only hope to win the prize
Laid up for him beyond the skies."

The Emperor wished the British Minister to bring before the notice of Her Majesty the Queen of England his appreciation of the splendid services which Gordon had rendered. He hoped that he would be rewarded in England as well as in China for his heroic achievements.

A subsequent letter in the *Times* said that Prince Kung, who was then the Regent of China, had waited upon Sir Frederick Bruce, and said to him, "You will be astonished to see me again, but I felt I could not allow you to leave without coming to see you about Gordon. We do not know what to do. He will not receive money from us, and we have already given him every honour which it is in the power of the Emperor to bestow; but as these are of little value in his eyes, I have brought you this letter, and I ask you to give it to the Queen of England that she may bestow on him some reward which would be more valuable in his eyes."

Sir Frederick Bruce sent this to London with a letter of his own:—"I enclose translation of a despatch from Prince Kung, containing the decree published by the Emperor, acknowledging the services of Gordon and requesting that Her Majesty's Government be pleased to recognise him. Gordon well deserves the favours of your Majesty for the skill and courage he has shown, his disinterestedness has elevated our national character in the eyes of the Chinese. Not only has he refused any pecuniary reward, but he has spent more than his pay in contributing to the comforts of the officers who served under him, and in assuaging the distress of the starving population whom he relieved from the yoke of their oppressors."

It does not appear that this letter was ever sent to the Queen, or noticed by the Government, and so the heroic deeds of a man of whom any nation might justly be proud, were forgotten.

CHAPTER III

"We are to relieve the distressed, to put the wanderer into his way, and to share our bread with the hungry, which is but the doing good to others."—Seneca.

Our hero having returned to his native land, and to settle for a little while at the quiet town of Gravesend, refused to be lionized, and he begged that no publication of his deeds of daring and devotion in China, should be recorded. His quiet life here as an engineer was not less remarkable, though of a different kind, than life in China had been. Here, however, he spent the energies of his spare time, to the services of the poor. At this juncture I was privileged to come in contact with this remarkable man, in the great city of Manchester, where for a few months, he was employed on some Governmental Commission. Like his Master Christ—he went about doing good. My position at this time was an agent, or scripture reader for "The Manchester City Mission." Gordon found his way to the office and saw the chairman of the mission, and from him got permission to accompany one of the missioners round his district. He expressed his desire to go round one of the poorest districts of the city; as it might afford him an opportunity of seeing for himself some of the social blots and scars in our national life; also of giving some practical help to the deserving poor. My district was such an one as would furnish him with the opportunities to satisfy him in that particular, and I was therefore asked to allow Col. Gordon to accompany me to its squalid scenes, to my Ragged School, cottage and open-air services, and to the sick and suffering, of which I had many on my list. This request was gladly complied with; for the first sight of the stranger made me love and trust him.

And now the hero of so many battles fought for freedom and liberty, was to witness scenes of warfare of a very different kind. War, it is true, but not where there are garments rolled in blood and victims slain; but war with the powers of darkness, war between good and evil, truth and error, light and darkness. We went together into the lowest slums of the district; walked arm in arm over the ground where misery tells its sad and awful tale, where poverty shelters its shivering frame, and where blasphemy howls its curse. We found out haunts of vice and sin, terrible in their character, and distressing in their consequences. I found he had not hitherto been accustomed to this kind of mission. Once on my entering a den of dangerous characters and lecturing them on their sinful course and warning them in unmistakable words of the consequences, he afterwards said: "I could not have found courage of the kind you show in this work; yet I never was considered lacking in courage on the field of battle. When in the Crimea, I was sent frequently and went on hands and knees through the fall of shells and the whizz of bullets right up to the Russian walls to watch their movements, and I never felt afraid; I confess I need courage to warn men of sin and its dangerous consequences." He met me, for a time almost daily, well supplied with tracts, which I noticed he used as a text for a few words of advice, or comfort, or warning as the case required, but he invariably left a silver coin between the leaves; this I think was a proof he was sincere in his efforts to do good. Along Old Millgate, and around the Cathedral, at that time, were numerous courts and alleys, obscure, often filthy, dark and dangerous; down or up these he accompanied me; up old rickety staircases, into old crumbling ruins of garrets he followed without hesitation.

At the bedside of the dying prodigal or prostitute he would sit with intense interest, pointing them to Him who casts out none. In our house to house visitation he would sit down and read of the Saviour's love, making special reference to those that are poor in this world, assuring them it was for the outcast and the forsaken, and the lost, that Jesus came to die. He would kneel down for prayer by a broken chair or the corner of a slop-stone, or by the wash-tub, and with the simplicity of a child, address in tender and touching petition, the Great Father of all in Heaven, while tears chased each other down his sun-tanned face; his great soul going out with his prayer for Heaven's blessing on the helpless poor.

His sympathy was tender as a child's, and his beneficence as liberal as the best of Christian's can be. He often came and took tea with me in my quiet home, where we had many very interesting interviews, and where we conversed on subjects varied but mostly religious; he rarely referred to his military achievements; when he did so it was with the greatest self abnegation and humility. He would say, "No honour belongs to me, I am only the instrument God uses to accomplish his purpose." I introduced him to my ragged school; this to him was a most interesting scene of work, and he volunteered to give us some of his time and service; and to see him with 20 or 30 of these ragged lads about him was to say the least, full of interest. He, however, had the happy art of getting at their heart at once; by incidents, stories and experiences, which compelled attention and confidence. In a very short time he won the esteem and the love of every lad in the school. To some of these lads he became specially attached, and for some time after he left Manchester he kept up with me, and with several of the lads, also with some of my colleagues on the mission—a very interesting correspondence. Happily, I have preserved a good number of these letters, and they show the spirit and motive of that noble soul, more than any poor words of mine can do.

Letter.

Gravesend,
June 19th, 1869.

"My Dear Mr. Wardle.—My long silence has not been because I had forgot you and your kind reception of me; but because secular work has so completely taken up my time of late. I was glad to hear of you . . . . and of the Dark Lane (ragged school) lads. I often wish I could go down with you and see them; I often think of them. I wish I could help them, but it is only by prayer that I can now benefit them. I loved them very much, and look forward to the time when our weary march, dogged by our great foe will be ended; and we meet for ever in our Heavenly home. I remember them all, Jones, Carr, &c., &c., and I often think of their poor young faces which must soon get deepened into wrinkles with sorrow and care. Thank God we go like Israel of old, after a new home; we cannot find our rest here! Day by day we are, little as we may think it, a day's march nearer, till someday we shall perhaps unexpectedly reach it."

Good bye, my dear Mr. Wardle,
Yours sincerely,
C. H. Gordon.

"Kind regards to *my* lads."

Gordon was deeply moved by the sights of poverty and distress around him; this was shown by the dress and appearance of the factory hands. He was especially struck by the clatter of the clogs—the Lancashire cotton operative's foot gear.

To his Sister he wrote:—

Manchester,
September 21st, 1867.

"Your heart would bleed to see the poor people, though they say there is no distress such as there was some time ago; they are indeed like sheep having no shepherd, but, thank God, though they look forlorn, they have a watchful and pitying eye upon them. It does so painfully affect me, and I do trust will make me think less of self, and more of these poor people. Little idea have the rich of other countries of the scenes in these parts. It does so make me long for that great day when He will come and put all things straight.

How long, O Lord, how long!

I have but little time to write by this post, so will say no more about that. I have less confidence in the flesh than ever, thank God, though it is a painful struggle and makes one long for the time when, this our earthly tabernacle, shall be dissolved; but may His will be done. If there is sin and misery, there is One who over-rules all things for good; we must be patient. The poor scuttlers here, male and female, fill me with sorrow. They wear wooden clogs, a sort of sabot, and make such a noise. Good-bye, and may God manifest Himself in all His power to all of you, and make you to rejoice with joy unspeakable. If we think of it, the only thing which makes the religion of our Lord Jesus Christ differ from that of every other religion, or profession, is this very indwelling of God the Holy Ghost in our bodies; we can do nothing good; Christ says, "Without me, ye can do nothing." You are dead in trespasses and sins, you are corpses, and must have life put in you, and that life is God Himself, who dwells in us, and shows us the things of Christ."

C. G. Gordon.

Letter. No. 2.

"My Dear Mr. Wardle,—I had a nice letter the other day from one of my lads, Carr, whom I hope you will look after, as well as all the rest. I have often thought of you all. Keep the "Tongue of Fire," [57] before you, and you will have great joy. I have thought much lately on the subject of God dwelling in us, and speaking through us. We are only witnesses, not judges; the Gospel is:—God loves you: not—Do you love God. The one is a witness, the other an inquiry which is not to be made by man of his fellow man, for it is impossible for man to love God unless he first feels and knows that God loves him. Our fault is, want of Charity one towards another. We do not go down to the poor lost sinner, but ask him to do what of himself he cannot do, viz., come up to us. What ought to be always floating in our proud hearts is:—'Who made thee to differ.'

Kind regards to all my friends.
Never forgotten, or to be forgotten.
Yours truly,
C. G. Gordon."

Letter. No. 3.

"My Dear Mr. Wardle, I send you 'Jukes on Genesis' and on the 'Four Gospels.' I have to send you his work on 'The Offerings in Leviticus,' and also Macintosh's 'Genesis and Exodus.' I am sure you will enjoy them. I cut Genesis up so as to lend it about; I hope you won't mind my having used them, and marked some papers. I hope D.V. to see you Monday evening, and with kind regards.

Believe me yours sincerely in Christ,
C. G. Gordon."

Gordon was intensely and deeply religious; it was in him certainly "as a well of water springing up into everlasting life." He could talk of nothing else, in whatever company, it was the same theme—"Christ in you the hope of glory." A favourite text of his was 1. John, chap. 4, ver. 15—"Whosoever shall confess that Jesus is the Son of God, God dwelleth in him, and he in God." This he took as a text for a little homily which he printed and circulated by thousands. After the above head-line, in special type, it ran thus:—"Reader! Do you confess that Jesus is the Son of God? Do you believe in your heart that Jesus is the Son of God? If you do then God dwells in you to-day. Whatever you are, whatever you have been, or have done,—and if you ask Him, 'O Lord, I believe that Jesus is the Son of God; show me, for His sake, that Thou livest in me.' He will make you feel His presence in your hearts, and will make you feel perfectly happy, which you cannot be in any other way. Many believe sincerely that Jesus is the Son of God, but are not happy, because they do not believe that which God tells them—that He lives in them both in body and soul, transforming the whole man into the likeness of Jesus Christ, if they confess Jesus to be His son. Do you believe this statement? If you do, yet do not feel God's presence, ask Him to show Himself to you, and He will surely do so."

After this homily, on the same tract, were the following passages of Scripture:—

> Luke, chap. 2, v. 13. "If ye then being evil, know how to give good gifts to your children; how much more shall your heavenly Father give the Holy Spirit to them that ask."
>
> Rom., chap. 10, v. 9. "If thou shall confess with thy mouth the Lord Jesus, and shalt believe in thine heart that God hath raised him from the dead, thou shalt be saved."
>
> I. Cor., chap. 3, v. 16. "Know ye not that ye are the temple of God, and that the Spirit of God dwelleth in you."
>
> I. Cor., chap. 6, v. 19. "Know ye not that your body is the temple of the Holy Ghost which is in you, which ye have of God, and ye are not your own."

II. Cor., chap. 6, v. 16. "Ye are the temple of the living God; as God hath said, I will dwell in them, and walk in them; and I will be their God, and they shall be my people."

The tone and spirit of this tract, is the kernel, if I may say so, of his deepest religious convictions.

He gave me a number of New Testaments for distribution, as he did also to one or two others of our missioners. The following letter accompanies the parcel:—

"My dear Mr. Wardle,—I have sent thirty Testaments for you and thirty for Mr. Fielden. Will you kindly oblige by marking in each the following passages, viz.:—

Matt. chap. 2, V. 28, 29. "Come unto me, all ye that labour and are heavy laden, and I will give you rest."

"Take my yoke upon you, and learn of me; for I am meek and lowly in heart; and ye shall find rest unto your souls."

Gal. ch. 5, v., 19., 25. "Now the works of the flesh are manifest, which are these: adultery, fornication, uncleanliness, lasciviousness, idolatry, witchcraft, hatred, variance, emulations, wrath, strife, seditions, heresies, 21. Envyings, murders, drunkenness, revellings, and such like; of the which I tell you before, as I have also told you in time past, that they which do such things shall not inherit the Kingdom of God." 22. But the fruit of the Spirit is love, joy, peace, long suffering, gentleness, goodness, faith, 23. Meekness, temperance; against such there is no law. 42. And they that are Christ's have crucified the flesh with the affections and lusts. If we live in the spirit, let us walk in the spirit."

Also I John ch. 4, v. 15. "Whosoever shall confess, etc."

He also published a little work entitled "Christ and His members; or the in-dwelling of God, the root of faith in Christ." One or two quotations may be sufficient to show the nature or scope of the work, a copy now lies before me.

"Belief or faith in Jesus being the Son of God, is the distinguishing spiritual mark of the members of Christ's body; it is a fruit which springs from a root, or source, from which it is sustained, and increased. This root is the indwelling of God the Holy Ghost in the soul. This indwelling gives faith or belief in the fact that even as the sun gives light, or the fire gives warmth, and as there can be no warmth without fire, and no light without the sun, neither can there be any belief in Jesus, without the indwelling of God in the soul."

He wrote me from Liverpool as follows:

> "My dear Mr. Wardle, do not forget to take the Testaments on Tuesday night. I always carry some with me, and always regret if I am taken by surprise, and have not any.
>
> Read and delight in "The tongue of fire," especially the first four or five chapters. If a man would be the instrument of winning souls to his Lord, it is utterly impossible for him to do so except through and by the Holy Ghost. He must be loving the praise of God, more than that of man. He must be humble, mean spirited it is called by many; even sometimes by his friends: and he can only be mean spirited by living near God. Let a man live distant from God, who is light, and he will not think he is so bad, but will think himself a little better than others, but let him live near God, and as he lives near Him he will feel himself worse than the worst; such is the power of the glorious light . . . . Goodbye; kind regards to all.

Yours sincerely, C. G. Gordon."

Another letter from Gravesend.

Nov. 24, 1868.

> "My dear Mr. Wardle, I thank you for your kind note. I send you 500 leaflets, kindly give them to the boys and girls of Buxton. The servant forgot to pay the carriage, so I send a small sum which I hope will cover it. I hear now and then of the Dark Lane Ragged School, from Mr. James Johnson, who kindly writes now and then. I will write (D.V.) again shortly. Kind regards.

Yours sincerely
C. G. Gordon."

Again he writes from Gravesend.

"My Dear Mr. Wardle, I hope you have not forgotten me, for I have not done so to you, but I am sure you are very busy, and hard worked . . . . Will you thank Fielden for his kind note and remember me to his wife and brother. Tell him I was very glad to hear of two of my boys, English and Hogg.

I often would like to look in and see you and the lads at *Dark Lane*, [63] and all my poor old sick folk I used to visit. Remember me to them all.

I do not see my way to come down yet awhile, for we have all our leave stopped. Excuse me for I have my hands full of work. Believe me, my dear Mr. Wardle.

Yours sincerely
C. G. Gordon."

CHAPTER IV

> "In the love of a brave and faithful man, there is always a strain of maternal tenderness; he gives out again those beams of protecting fondness, which were shed on him as he lay upon his mother's knee."—Geo. Elliott.

A son of one of our missionaries (J. Johnson) says of Gordon "he was one of the most unassuming and gentle men I ever met; and I well remember his saintly conversation, as he sat at tea with us. I also remember, (though only a youth) being struck with his humility, especially for one of his rank and profession. He generally had on a well worn greyish overcoat, the side pockets of which gaped somewhat with constant usage for into them he would cram a large number of tracts and sally forth in company with me or another of the missionaries, or as sometimes happened he went alone, drop a tract here or there and speak a seasonable word. He spoke to me as a youth, as some of our saintly old pastors used to do to the children of the penniless where they stayed. He wrote me occasionally. A specimen I herewith append."

Letter to Mr. Johnson, junr.:

> "My dear J. . . . since we had a few words together you have not been out of my mind for any length of time together, and I was very glad to hear of you to-day from your father. God acts in mysterious ways and He gave me comfort concerning you on that evening. Trust Him with all thine heart. He says (He who cannot lie) He lives in you if you believe that Jesus is the Son of God. His word is truth whatever may be our feelings, which change as the clouds. You are my dear friend, saved not on account of your feelings, but because our blessed Lord loved you unto death, and has washed you in His own blood . . . . I will not write more than express my hope that He who has begun a good work may perfect it. Yea he surely will, for He says He will perfect that which concerneth us—make you useful in His service. May He strengthen you to fight the good fight of faith, and give you that crown of glory which fadeth not away; I am very sure He will. May His will be done on this poor sorrowing world,

for the longer we live the more fleeting are its glories. Good-bye, my dear young friend. Believe me

Yours sincerely
C. G. Gordon."

Also a further letter to Mr. Johnson. This was written during my illness and leave of absence from duty—

"My dear Mr. Johnson, I have received your letter with many thanks. I am so much obliged for your letting me know of my lads, and have written to them a few lines. I wish sometimes I was with you. I like your quiet earnestness; there is little of that here, and I like the work; I have also said a few words to your son; the Holy Ghost is the teacher for Him, and will not leave His work till he is happy.

I hope Mr. Wardle is improving in health. "And he shall sit as a refiner and purifier of silver." Silver is spoilt if heated too much, therefore the refiner sits watching; until it is purified when the refiner sees his image reflected in its surface; so with us, our Lord will see that we are not too much heated, only just enough to reflect His image. Will you thank Mr. Fielden for his kind letter, I quite feel for his trials in that district, but he has a fellow helper and worker in his kind Lord who feels for him and will support him through all. Give my kind regard to Spence, your wife and son, and to all my friends.

And believe me my dear Mr. Johnson,

Yours sincerely,
C. G. Gordon."

Mr. Johnson writes:—

"One evening after I had been observing his patient endurance and perseverance with one of the reckless, insolent lads as we left the school, I, in a quiet pleasant way remarked "I fear Colonel, your Christian work in Dark Lane Ragged School will never get the fame and applause from this world that your military achievements in China have lately secured for you."

> "My dear Sir," he replied "If I can but be the means in the hands of God of leading any of these precious sons to Jesus, I must place that amongst the most glorious trophies of my life, and to hear the Master at last say 'Inasmuch as ye have done it to one of the least of these, ye have done it unto Me,' will be to me a resplendent undying glory when so many of earth's fleeting honours have tarnished."
>
> "It is impossible (says Lord Blatchford about General Gordon) to imagine a man more completely in the presence of God, or more absolutely careless of his own distinction, comfort, wealth or life. A man unreservedly devoted to the cause of the oppressed. One bows before him as before a man of a superior order of things." Mr. Boulger says, "There will never be another Gordon." Sir William Butler said of him, "He was unselfish as Sydney; of courage, dauntless as Wolfe; of honour, stainless as Outram; of sympathy, wide-reaching as Drummond; of honesty, straightforward as Napier; of faith, as steadfast as Moore."

We believe Gordon answered to all these encomiums and well deserved them.

Edgmont Hake, writing of him says:—"He lived wholly for others; his home at Gravesend was school, hospital, church, and almshouse all in one. His work more like that of a Home missionary than of a military officer. The troubles of all interested him alike, but he had a warm corner in his heart for lads." This will be seen from letters produced. Many of the lads he rescued from the slums and gutters; he cleaned them, clothed them, fed them, and gave them shelter and home, sometimes for weeks and even longer. He taught in the evenings lessons suitable to their conditions; not forgetting the moral and spiritual side of his work. And he did this work without fee or reward, and he did it with all his heart. He was as enthusiastic about this duty as he was about his military duties. He called these lads *"His kings."*

Leigh Hunt's ideal of a king describes very closely Gordon's ideal:—

"'Tis not the wealth that makes a king
Nor the purple colouring,
Nor a brow that's bound with gold,
Nor gate on mighty hinges rolled;
That king is he who void of fear,
Can look abroad with bosom clear,
Who can tread ambition down,

Nor be swayed by smile nor frown,
Nor for all the treasure cares,
That mine conceals or harvest wears,
Or that golden sands deliver,
Bosomed on a glassy river,
Safe with wisdom for his crown,
He looks on all things calmly down,
He has no fear of earthly thing,
This is it that makes a king,
And all of us who e'er we be
May carve us out such royalty."

On one occasion a lad in the employ of a Gravesend tradesman was discovered to have been pilfering on a somewhat serious scale. When the fact was proved beyond question, the master declared he would have the boy punished by imprisonment. The mother of the boy, hearing of this sad affair, was almost broken-hearted, and at her wit's end. Someone who had heard of Gordon's love for lads, also his intense desire to help all in trouble, suggested that she should see him and explain her case. So, with all a mother's earnestness, she went at once to Gordon and told him the whole story, and begged with tears for his sympathy and help. After hearing the story his heart was touched, he could not refuse a mother's appeal. When a mother pleads, there is power and pathos difficult for any to withstand, much less Gordon. So he went to the lad's late employer, and after considerable argument, the master undertook not to prosecute, but only on condition that Gordon would personally undertake to look after the lad himself, for one year at least. This Gordon promised, and he took the boy to his own home, sent him to a good school at his own expense for the year; then he got him a good situation on board one of Her Majesty's vessels. That lad became a man of honour and respectability, secured good situations, won for himself a good character, and the mother and the sailor boy in their heart often blessed Gordon, who saved the boy from prison, ruin and disgrace, and the mother from a broken heart. His rescue work amongst boys was work he loved supremely, in it he found his highest joys. His pleasures were not secured where many seek them, viz., at the theatre, at the gambling-house, at the racecourse, at the public-house, or in accumulating wealth, or in winning renown and glory—these were nothing to Gordon. To save a fallen lad, was to him the highest gratification; in this work he was very successful.

Many a rescued lad was he able to restore to his home and to society, and to the world. For many of these lads he was able to secure situations on board ship. To show his interest in them when away he had a large map on his study wall, in this map were pins in very many places. These, he told a visitor, showed the position of the ships on which his lads were located; and he moved the pins as the ships moved and prayed for each boy from day to day. The workhouse and the infirmary were places he used to visit, and his visits were remembered by the inmates, as all the fruits and flowers he could grow were given to these places and to the sick and poor whom he visited. Very often the dying sent for him in preference to a clergyman, and he was, if at home, always ready; no matter what the weather or what the distance. His works were essentially works of charity, and these were not done to be seen of men. He was one of the humblest men I ever met. He would not occupy the chair at a meeting or even go on to the platform. Once I remember he addressed a gathering after tea of those who had been rescued and who were likely to be useful to others, but he would not be lionised or praised. He would say, "No; I am but the instrument: the praise belongs to God." His spirit was the fruitful cause of all the work he did.

"Give me that lowest place,
Not that I dare ask for that lowest place.
But Thou hast died that I might share
Thy glory by Thy side.
Give me that lowest place, or if for me
That lowest place too high
Make one more low, where I may sit
And see my God; and love Thee so."

He recognised "that pure religion and undefiled before God the Father is this, to visit the fatherless, and the widows in their affliction, and to keep unspotted from the world." This kindled his enthusiasm, influenced his chivalrous character, and we think had largely to do with his success. To know him was to know a Christian, a Christlike man—God's man.

With Job (ch. 29, verses 11, 12, etc.) he could say truly—

> "When the ear heard me, then it blessed me; when the eye saw me, it gave witness to me. Because I delivered the poor that cried and the fatherless, and him that had none to help him. The blessing of him that was ready to perish came upon me: and I caused the widow's heart to sing for joy. I was eyes to the blind and feet was I to the lame. I was a father to the poor, and the cause which I knew not I searched out."

He could truly say

"I live for those that love me:
For those that know me true;
For the heaven that smiles above me
And waits my coming too.
For the cause that needs assistance,
For the wrong that needs resistance.
For the future in the distance,
And for the good that I can do."

Upon his removal from Gravesend in 1873 a local newspaper writing of his removal, and deploring his loss, said—"Our readers will hear with regret of the departure of Colonel Gordon from the town, in which he has resided for six years; gaining a name for the most exquisite charity that will long be remembered. Nor will he be less missed than remembered, for in the lowest walks of life he has been so unwearied in well-doing that his departure will be felt as a terrible calamity. His charity was essential charity, having its root in deep philanthropic feeling and goodness, and always shunning the light of publicity." Many were the friends who grieved over his departure from Gravesend, for they ne'er would look upon his like again.

CHAPTER V

> "If a man do not erect in this age his own tomb e'er he dies, he shall live no longer in monuments than the bell rings and his widow weeps."—Shakespeare.

A new chapter now opens in our story of Gordon. Sir Samuel Baker had resigned the honoured position of Governor General of the Soudan. Gordon was selected as the man who, of all others, was most suitable for such an appointment. Our Government acquiesced in the Khedive's offer of this post to Gordon, so he accepted the responsible position.

The Khedive offered him, it is stated, a salary £10,000 per annum; this, however, he refused to accept. He said "Your Majesty I cannot accept it, as I should look upon it as the life's blood wrung out of those poor people over whom you wish me to rule." "Name your own terms then," said the Khedive. "Well," replied Gordon, "£2,000 per annum I think will keep body and soul together, what should I require more than this for." About the close of the year 1873 he left his country and loved ones behind him, for that lone sad land, with its ancient history. We think Gordon played such a part that his name will be honourably associated with Egypt, and remembered from generation to generation.

I am indebted to the author of *Gordon in Central Africa* for the following abstract of the Khedive's final instructions to Col. Gordon, dated Feb. 16th, 1874.

> "The province which Colonel Gordon has undertaken to organise and to govern is but little known. Up to the last few years, it had been in the hands of adventurers who had thought of nothing but their own lawless gains, and who had traded in ivory and slaves. They established factories and governed them with armed men. The neighbouring tribes were forced to traffic with them whether they liked it or not. The Egyptian Government, in the hope of putting an end to this inhuman trade had taken the factories into their own hands, paying the owners an indemnification.

Some of these men, nevertheless, had been still allowed to carry on trade in the district, under a promise that they would not deal in slaves. They had been placed under the control of the Governor of the Soudan. His authority, however, had scarcely been able to make itself felt in these remote countries. The Khedive had resolved therefore to form them into a separate government, and to claim as a monopoly of the State, the whole of the trade with the outside world. There was no other way of putting an end to the slave trade which at present was carried on by force of arms in defiance of law. When once brigandage had become a thing of the past, and when once a breach had been made in the lawless customs of long ages, then trade might be made free to all. If the men who had been in the pay of adventurers were willing to enter the service of the Government, Col. Gordon was to make all the use of them he could. If on the other hand they attempted to follow their old course of life, whether openly or secretly, he was to put in force against them to the utmost severity of martial law. Such men as these must find in the Governor neither indulgence, nor mercy. The lesson must be made clear even in those remote parts that a mere difference of colour does not turn men into wares, and that life and liberty are sacred things."

Another object of the new Governor should be to establish a line of posts through all his provinces, so that from one end to the other they might be brought into direct communication with Khartoum. Those posts should follow, as far as was possible, the line of the Nile; but for a distance of seventy miles the navigation of that river was hindered by rapids. He was to search out the best way of overcoming this hindrance, and to make a report thereon to the Khedive.

In dealing with the *Chieftains* of the tribes which dwelt on the shores of the lakes, the Governor was above all to try to win their confidence. He must respect their territory, and conciliate them by presents, and whatever influence he gains over them, he must use in the endeavour to persuade them to put an end to the wars, which they so often make on each other in the hope of carrying off slaves. Much tact would be needed, for should he succeed in stopping the slave trade, while wars were still waged among the chiefs, it might well come to pass that, for want of a market, the prisoners would, in such a case, be slaughtered. Should he find it needful to exercise a real control over any of these tribes, it will be better to leave to the chieftains the direct government. Their obedience must be secured by making them dread his power.

He made the journey to Khartoum without any mishap or serious difficulty, reaching there in May, 1874, and was installed in office on the fifth. A royal salute from the government house guns was fired in honour of this event; the new Governor-General was, of course, expected to make a speech, after the order of his predecessors. But all he said was, "With the help of God I will hold the balance level." This was received with the greatest enthusiasm, for it evidently pleased the people more than if he had addressed them for an hour. His attention was soon directed towards the poverty-stricken and helpless people all around him. He caused special enquiries to be made; then he began to distribute his gifts of charity to all who he believed were really in need; and in three days he had given away one thousand pounds of his first year's salary. He had not been long in the Soudan before he realized the tremendous responsibilities he had assumed; and with all his strength of character, and his trust in his Almighty, ever-present Friend, it is not to be wondered at that when alone in the trackless desert, with the results of ages of wrong-doing before him, this man of heroic action and indomitable spirit sometimes gave way to depression and murmuring; although this was exceedingly rare. If we remember what he had already done and suffered for down-trodden humanity. And that now he was doing heroic work for the true hero's wages—the love of Christ, and the good of his fellow-men. He was labouring not for himself, but as the hand of God in providence, in the faith that his work was of God's own appointing. The wonder is that in the face of perils so dangerous, work so difficult, and sufferings so intense, that his spirit was not completely crushed and broken. We must bear in mind, his work there was to secure peace to a country that appeared to be bent on war; to suppress slavery amongst a people to whom it was a second nature, and to whom the trade in human flesh was life, and honour, and fortune. To make and discipline an army out of the rawest recruits ever put in the field, to develop and grow a flourishing trade, and to obtain a fair revenue, amid the wildest anarchy in the world; the immensity of the undertaking, the infinity of detail involved in a single step toward this end, the countless odds to be faced; the many pests, the deadly climate, the nightly and daily alternations of overpowering heat, and of bitter cold, to be endured and overcome; the environment of bestial savagery, and ruthless fanaticism;—all these contributed to make the achievement unique in human history. He was face to face with evil in its worst form, and saw it in all its appalling effects upon the nation and its people. He seemed to have everything against him, and to be utterly alone.

There stood in front of him the grim ruined land. He faced it, however, as a saint and soldier should do; he stood for right, truth, and for God.

GORDON ON HIS FAVOURITE CAMEL.

"He would dare to do right. Dare to be true
He had a work that no other could do;
He would do it so wisely, so bravely, so well,
That angels might hasten the story to tell."

After some time he writes:—

"How the Khedive is towards me I don't know, but thank God he prevents me caring for any one's favour or disfavour. I honestly say I do not know anyone who would endure the exile and worries of my position out here. Some might fear if they were dismissed, that the world would talk. Thank God! I am screened from that fear. I know that I have done my best, as far as my intellect would allow me, for the Khedive, and have tried to be just to all."

On contemplating retirement, he writes:—

"Now imagine what I lose by coming back, if God so wills it; a life in a tent, with a cold humid air at night, to which if, from the heat of the tent you expose yourself, you will suffer for it, either in liver or elsewhere. The most ordinary fare. *Most* ordinary I can assure you; no vegetables, dry biscuits, a few bits of broiled meat, and some dry macaroni, boiled in water and sugar. I forgot some soup; up at dawn and to bed between eight and nine p.m. No books but one, and that not often read for long, for I cannot sit down for a study of those mysteries. All day long, worrying about writing orders, to be obeyed by others in the degree as they are near or distant from me: obliged to think of the veriest trifle, even to the knocking off the white ants from the stores, etc.—that is one's life; and, speaking materially, for what gain? At the end of two years, say £2,000. At the end of three say £3,500 at the outside. The gain to be called 'His Excellency,' and this money. Yet his poor 'Excellency' has to slave more than any individual; to pull ropes, to mend this; make a cover to that (just finished a capital cover to the duck Gun). I often say, 'drop the excellency, and do this instead.'"

Again he writes:—

"This country would soon cure a man of his ambition, I think, and make him content with his lot. The intense heat, and other stagnation except you have some disagreeable incident, would tame the most enthusiastic; a thin, miserable tent under which you sit, with the perspiration pouring off you. A month of this life, and you would be dissatisfied with your lot."

Gordon had kept up some very interesting correspondence with an old friend in China; an old officer in Gordon's "Ever victorious Army," Li Hung Chang. While Gordon is feeling unwell, and disposed to send his resignation to the Khedive—he writes in his journal:—

July 21st, 1879.

"I shall (D.V.) leave for Cairo in ten days, and I hope to see you soon; but I may have to go to Johannis before I go to

> Cairo. I am a wreck, like the portion of the 'Victory' towed into Gibraltar after Trafalgar; but God has enabled me, or rather has used me, to do what I wished to do—that is, break down the slave trade. "Those that honour me I will honour." May I be ground to dust, if He will glorify Himself in me; but give me a humble heart, for then he dwells there in comfort. I wrote you a letter about my illness and tore it up. Thank God, I am pretty well now, but I have passed the grave once lately, and never thought to see Khartoum. The new Khedive is more civil, but I no longer distress myself with such things. God is the sole ruler, and I try to walk sincerely before Him."

The letter from Li Hung Chang was to him a source of great satisfaction and pleasure, as it showed his example had affected for good this eastern ambassador, who visited this country only a very few years ago.

The letter ran thus:—

Tientsin,
March 22nd, 1879.

> "To His Excellency Colonel C. G. Gordon,
> Khartoum, Egypt.
>
> "Dear Sir.—I am instructed by his Excellency the Grand Secretary, Li, to answer your esteemed favour, dated the 27th October, 1878, from Khartoum, which was duly received. I am right glad to hear from you. It is now fourteen years since we parted from each other. Although I have not written to you, I often speak of you, and remember you with very great interest. The benefit you have conferred on China does not appear with your person, but is felt throughout the regions in which you played so important and active a part. All those people bless you for the blessings of peace and prosperity which they now enjoy.
>
> Your achievements in Egypt are well known throughout the civilized world. I see often in the papers of your noble works on the Upper Nile. You are a man of ample resources, with which you suit yourself to any emergency. My hope is that you may long be spared to improve the conditions of the people amongst whom your lot is cast. I am striving hard to advance my people to a higher state of development, and to

unite both this and all other nations within the 'Four seas' under one common brotherhood.

I wish you all manner of happiness and prosperity. With my highest regards,

I remain,
Yours truly,
Li Hung Chang."

In all, and through all these various trying vicissitudes he remained true to his innate religious convictions, and looked upon it all as the filling in of a plan, which was divine. His hours for prayer were maintained with as great a regularity as were those of another eastern official servant, Daniel, who "three times a day kneeled on his knees and prayed and gave thanks to God." Gordon, when at prayer, placed outside his tent a white handkerchief, this was the sign the Governor was at his devotions, and no servant or messenger must disturb him. He kept closely in touch with God, so to speak. His outer life might be ruffled by storms and tempests, but within he had the perfect peace.

While Gordon was hoping to get away from the trying climate and yet more trying circumstances around him, a message (not unexpected) reached him, giving him instructions to proceed to Abyssinia, and see if he could settle the dispute or misunderstanding that had arisen between Johannis the King and the Khedive. He proceeded on that very risky mission as he states in his letters; the journey was "indescribable in its solitary grandeur. These interminable deserts, and arid mountain passes fill the heart with far different thoughts than civilized lands do." With few attendants, he writes:—"We are still slowly crawling over the world's crust. Reaching the dominions of the King of Abyssinia, we camped near Ras Alonla, and the priests used to gather at 3 a.m. in knots of two and three and chant for an hour in a wild melodious manner the Psalms of David. Awakened at this unearthly hour no one could help being impressed. Some of them had children who chanted." Again he writes:—"We have just passed a famous convent. The great high priest, who only comes out to meet the King, and who is supposed to be the King's right hand in religious questions, came out to meet us. I had some splendid silk brocade, which I gave him. He held a gold cross in his hand, and spoke of the love of Christ. He seemed to be a deeply religious man."

Father Soho says of Abyssinia:—

"No country in the world is so full of churches, monasteries, and ecclesiastics, as Abyssinia. It is hardly possible to sing in one church, or monastery, without being heard in another, and perhaps by several. They sing the Psalms of David, of which they have a very exact translation in their own language. They begin their concert by stamping their feet on the ground, and playing gently on their instruments; but when have become warm by degrees, they leave off drumming, and fall to leaping, dancing, shouting and clapping hands, till their is neither tune nor pause, but rather a religious riot. For this manner of religious worship, they quote the Psalm—"O clap your hands, all ye nations." Gordon says, "I could not but like this poor simple-minded peasantry."

Again he writes:—

"We are about a days march from the river Taczzi, which joins the Nile at Berber. Nearing the Palace, if so I may call it, I was met by the King's body guard. I was of course wearing the Crest and Field Marshal's uniform; the soldiers were sitting on their heels and never got up. Passing through them I found my mule so tired that I got down and walked. On arrival at the Palace, I was admitted to the King, who sat upon a raised däis, with the Itagè, or Chief Priest on the ground at his left hand. Then guns were fired, and the King said, "That is in your honour, and you can retire," which I did, to see him again shortly. Again Gordon visited the Royal personage, and was granted permission to present his case, but Gordon considered himself unduly humbled as he was ordered to stand afar off; a stool at length was placed for him to sit upon. This humble position Gordon would at other times have accepted and tolerated, but not here and now; he must show his dignity as the representative of a Foreign, powerful monarch; he seized the stool and carried it up to near where the King sat, and placed it by his side, saying, "Though in your hands I may be a prisoner, I am a man as much as you are, and can only meet you as an equal." His sable Majesty was greatly annoyed at Gordon's audacious conduct, and remarking said, "Gordon Pasha don't you know I am the King, and could kill you if I wished." "I am perfectly aware of that," said Gordon, "Do so at once if it is your Royal pleasure, I am ready." "What," said the King, "Ready to be killed?" "Certainly," said Gordon, "I am always ready to die, and so far from fearing you putting me to death, you would confer a favour on me by so doing, for you would be doing for me that which I am precluded by my religious convictions from doing for myself. You would relieve me from all the troubles the future may have in store for me." "Then my power has no terror for you, Gordon!" "None whatever," he replied. So Gordon proved more than a match for this half-civilized Abyssinian King. His visit, however, could not be considered successful as his Majesty was unreasonable in all his demands, and so put out of the power of Gordon to reach any settlement. So he left the King without effecting what he came to do. How to get away now was to him a source of anxiety. As he surmised, they were not likely to allow him to carry back the valuables he had in his possession. It required all his tact and wit and discretion in this perilous position. He, however, at the cost of about £1,400 in bribes and gifts, managed to get away. Then he had to find his way back alone. This was a severe ordeal. Over mountains covered with snow, and through defiles of rocky places, now meeting with wild hordes of the dog-faced baboons, then with the uncivilized tribes of the human species none the less dangerous. He, however, by the care of an ever watchful Providence, had escaped serious harm and reached Khartoum in safety."

CHAPTER VI

"There is no death, what seems so is transition.
This life of mortal breath is but the suburb of the life Elysian,
Whose portals we call Death."—Longfellow.

Gordon had felt for some time uneasy in his position, as the under officials looked upon him as a religious fanatic, and too strict to govern; they tried to annoy him, and they succeeded: so he sent in his resignation to the Khedive, and as soon as he could conveniently, he turned his face homeward.

First of course he visited the Khedive, and he received from him a princely welcome, being addressed by him in these words: "I am glad to see you Gordon Pasha again amongst us, and have great pleasure in once more personally acknowledging the loyalty with which you always served my country, and my government. I should very much like you to remain in my service, but if you must retire from us, as you say you must, then I am reluctantly compelled to accept your resignation. I regret, my dear Gordon, to lose so valued a counsellor and friend, and the hearty co-operation of so useful a servant: and in parting from you, I desire to express my sincere thanks to you; assuring you that my remembrance of you and of your services to this country will never be forgotten."

Gordon was greatly in need of the rest he now seemed to have secured by his resignation. His over sensitive nature could not have borne up much longer; a frame of iron must have gone under in such circumstances; for on his own individual shoulders he carried each man's burden, causing him days of anxiety and nights of unrest. At Alexandria he was examined by Dr. MacKie the surgeon to the British Consulate, who certified that he was "suffering from symptoms of nervous exhaustion. I have recommended him (the Dr. adds) to retire for several months for complete rest, and quiet—and that he may be able to enjoy fresh and wholesome food, as I consider much of this illness is the result of continued bodily fatigue, anxiety and indigestible food. I have strongly insisted on his abstaining from all exciting work—especially such as implies business or political excitement." Splendid advice, but would Gordon follow it? Could his active life be suppressed even for so short a time? None find it harder to rest than those who need it most. Gordon had often thought of what pleasure in rest he would find when his retirement was an accomplished fact. He would lie in bed until dinner. He would take short walks after dinner. He would undertake no long journeys, either driving or by railway. He would not be tempted to go to dinner parties. He would really have a quiet time; it was, however, only for a short period.

The private secretaryship to Lord Ripon was vacant, and it was offered to Gordon; he accepted it, but on landing at Bombay he found the position would not be to his liking. He says of Lord Ripon, "we parted perfect friends." After Gordon left Egypt someone there wrote to our press saying, "The name of Gordon whenever and wherever mentioned sends a thrill of admiration and love throughout the vast Soudan territory. For a hand so strong, yet withal so beneficent, has never before ruled the peoples of this unhappy country." Gordon left the Soudan peaceful, prosperous and happy, comparatively. After his resignation of the position of private secretary to Lord Ripon, he was invited to visit China again by Mr. Hart, Chinese Commissioner of Customs at Pekin, who said to Gordon, "I am directed to invite you here (that is to say China). Please come and see for yourself. This opportunity for doing really useful work on a large scale ought not to be lost: work, position, conditions can all be arranged with yourself here to your satisfaction. Do take six months leave and come." It was characteristic of Gordon that he replied as follows:—"Inform Hart, Gordon will leave for Shanghai first opportunity; as for the conditions, Gordon is indifferent."

He applied to our Government for leave of absence on the grounds that he was invited to go to China. They asked him to state more particularly what for, and what position he was intending to fill. "I am ignorant" was his reply. This was not considered satisfactory and leave was refused. He, however, sent his resignation to the War Office, and proceeded to China. Reaching the flowery land, once more he proceeded from Shanghai to Tientsin and there he had an interview with his old friend and companion in arms, Li Hung Chang. From him he learned the condition in which national and political matters stood. His stay in China was not very prolonged, but his influence was felt in the Councils of the Empire; and when he left he knew that peace prevailed, and that the war between Russia and China had been averted. In the meantime things in the Soudan began to give trouble, the cloud on the horizon gathered in blackness. Almost immediately Gordon left the Soudan the Turkish Pashas began their plundering, robbing and ill-treating the poor Soudanese so much that we cannot wonder at the rising of the natives in favour of the Madhi, for the latter was promising them deliverance from this cruel oppression. The rule of the Pashas and Bashi-Ba-Zoucks, the Duke of Argyle declared to be "cruel, intolerant, and unbearable."

Colonel Stewart, in his report, stated that "he believed not one half of the taxes wrung from these poor people ever found their money go into the treasury of the Khedive." They were taxed and levied so unjustly and unmercifully that whole districts were reduced to absolute destitution. The general rising of the natives against this dire oppression, threw them into the arms of the Madhi. He very soon had a most powerful following, and he quickly mobilized an army that in 1882 was believed to number not less than 200,000 fighting men. In July of that year this boastful usurper pushed his forces into conflict with the Egyptians, when the latter were worsted with terrible loss. About 6,000 of their bravest men were either killed in battle or left wounded on the field and the remainder were routed. Shortly after another great battle followed. This also went in favour of the usurper, and a loss of 10,000 men inflicted. One engagement followed another and all went to show that the Madhi had won the sympathy and support of the masses of the people, and it appeared likely he would soon have undisputed sway over the entire Soudan. Still another effort was to be made to hurl back this powerful and persistent foe. Hicks Pasha, "a brave leader," "a noble general," with an army of 10,000 men, with 6,000 camels, a large number of pack horses and mules, was sent to arrest the advance of this desperate foe. For some time no news reached us, as he was shut out from all means of communication with the outer world. At length the appalling news came, not only of his defeat, but of his utter destruction. One man only was known to have escaped to tell the tale. He states, "We were led by a treacherous guide into a mountain pass or defile, and there shut in by rocks; we were confronted and surrounded by probably 100,000 of the enemy. For three days and nights the battle raged; the few British officers fought like lions against these overwhelming odds, until, so completely cut up by sword, bullet and spear, that he feared he was the only man who managed to escape." This large army was literally annihilated—1,200 officers perished in this one battle. The Madhi took 17,000 Remington rifles, 7 Krupp guns, 6 Nordenfelts, 29 brass mounted cannon, and a very large amount of ammunition. So that he appeared to be master of the situation. "What next for the Soudan?" was being everywhere asked in Egypt and in the Soudan. "Oh that Gordon was here," was the cry of many of the poor down-trodden Soudanese. They believed him to be the only man who could bring peace to their desolate and unhappy country.

Gordon was at that time taking a quiet rest near Jaffa, in the Holy Land, and making investigations into places specially spoken of in the

Scriptures. He thought he could locate the place where Samuel took Agag and hewed him to pieces. Also the well, called "Jacob's Well," and other places of interest. It is said at this juncture, things in the Soudan had become hopeless. A gentleman sent to one of the papers at Cairo the following message: "Would to God that an angel would stand at the elbow of Lord Granville in London, and say, And now send men to Joppa, and call for one Gordon, and he shall tell thee what thou oughtest to do." Strange to say, about this time, Gordon was sent for to London, where he had interviews with Lord Hartington, Secretary of State for War, Lord Granville, Minister for Foreign Affairs, Lord Northbrook, First Lord of the Admiralty, and Sir Charles Dilke, President of the Local Government Board, at the War Office, and in a very short space of time, the question, which was destined to have far reaching results, was settled, and Gordon declared his willingness to go to Khartoum at the earliest possible date. Indeed he said, "At once," and to go alone.

Something like the following conversation is said to have taken place between Gordon and one of his very intimate friends: "Well, General, have you got your kit ready?" His reply was, "I have got what I always have: this hat is good enough, so are these clothes, my boots I think are strong enough." "And how are you off for cash?" "Ah! I was nearly forgetting that. I had to borrow £25 from the King of the Belgians to bring me home from Palestine; this I must repay, and I shall of course need a little more for common daily use." "How much do you think, two or three thousand pounds?" "Oh dear no! One hundred pounds apiece for myself and Stewart, will be enough; what on earth should we want so much money for." And so the gallant general, with his faithful companion—the late lamented Colonel Stewart, started.

We are told they were accompanied to Charing Cross railway station by H. R. H. the Duke of Cambridge, who took their tickets for them; also by Lord Wolseley (who would insist on carrying Gordon's portmanteau), Colonel Brackenbury, and Lord Hartington's private secretary, who bade them good-bye, and God speed on their mission, from which they were never to return. We think history will never record a more heroic example of patriotism, than that of this God-fearing officer, riding forth upon his swift footed camel, with only one English friend and companion, the Colonel Stewart, and a few Arab attendants, to confront and settle the wild and barbarous hordes of the Madhi.

One of our papers published the following appropriate lines:—

"Not with an army at command,
Not fenced about with guns and swords,
But trusting to their single hands,
Amid a host of savage hordes,
The hero Gordon wends in haste,
Across the desert's arid waste,
Beset with perils lies his way,
Yet fear he knows not: Nelson like,
His life would be an easy prey,
If but the Arab dare to strike.
But over him there hangs a spell,
The Soudan people know full well:
Oft he had taught the Eastern mind
The grace of noble-hearted deeds;
Oft cast abuses to the wind,
And succoured men in direst needs;
Nor shall the charm that all allow
Is grandly his, forsake him now:
Oh! should the power of his name
Bend the false prophet to its thrall
And make him deem the hero came,
To pay him just a friendly call,
The ruthless carnage soon might cease,
And Egypt be again at peace."

The subject of Gordon's mission came up several times in the British House of Commons as might be expected. Sir Stafford Northcote on one occasion said—"There is one point upon which all our minds are fixed—I mean the mission of General Gordon. On that point I was anxious to say little or nothing. General Gordon is now engaged in an attempt of the most gallant and dangerous kind. No one can speak with too much admiration of his courage and self-devotion: no one can fail, in this country to sympathise with him, and earnestly desire his safety and success."

Reaching Cairo, Gordon received his plans and instructions from the Khedive, and here we think arose some of the complications and misunderstandings as to his actual position. Was he in the employ of the Khedive, or was he still responsible to the Home Government? The Khedive expressed himself to Gordon in a letter dated Jan. 26, 1884.

"Excellency,—You are aware that the object of your arrival here, and of your mission to the Soudan is to carry into execution the evacuation of those territories, and to withdraw our troops, civil officials, and such of the inhabitants, together with their belongings, as may wish to leave for Egypt. We trust that your Excellency will adopt the most effective measures for the accomplishment of your mission in this respect, and that, after completing the evacuation, you will take the necessary steps for establishing an organized Government in the different provinces of the Soudan, for the maintenance of order, and the cessation of disasters, and incitement to revolt. We have full confidence in your tried abilities and tact, and are convinced that you will accomplish your mission according to your desire."

This was hardly in harmony with a telegram from Lord Granville who said that "*undertaking military expeditions was beyond the scope of the Commission he held, and at variance with the pacific policy which was the purpose of his mission to the Soudan.*" Between the Khedive's instructions and commission to Gordon, and his holding commission as an officer of the Crown, Gordon was in a very difficult position, and those who have blamed Mr. Gladstone, for what they may have been pleased to call "desertion of Gordon," should acquaint themselves with all the circumstances of the case before doing so, and when all is known, such blame will be withheld.

Gordon, without lingering in Cairo, hastened to cross the desert and get to Khartoum as quickly as possible. Thus our hero went forth with a gallantry never surpassed, if ever equalled. He rode his camel across that land of storm and drought, trusting only in Him, who had so often "covered his defenceless head, beneath the shadow of His wing."

CHAPTER VII

"Not all who seem to fail have failed indeed,
Not all who fail have therefore worked in vain;
There is no failure for the good and wise;
What though the seed should fall by the way-side,
And the birds snatch it; yet the birds are fed,
Or they may bear it far across the tide
To give rich harvests after thou art dead."

Kingsley.

Sir E. Baring wired to Lord Granville, "The interview between Gordon and the Khedive was very satisfactory." Again—"Gordon leaves Cairo in good spirits."

His arrival at Khartoum, it is stated, was marked by wonderful demonstrations of welcome by the people; thousands of them pressing towards him to kiss his feet: calling him the "Sultan of the Soudan." His first speech was received with the wildest enthusiasm. He said, "I come not with soldiers but with God on my side, to redress the wrongs of the Soudan." The day after he held a levee at the palace, when vast multitudes thronged around him, kissing the ground on which he walked, calling him "Father," "Sultan," "Saviour." He appreciated highly their apparent loyalty and devotion, and he had offices opened at once where everyone who had a grievance might bring it, have it heard and judged.

The Government books recording the outstanding debts of the over-taxed people, *were publicly burned in the presence of thousands of onlookers; the kourbasher, whips, and implements of torture were thrown down upon the blazing pile*: thus the evidence of debts, and the emblems of oppression perished together in the presence of an almost frenzied people! Next Gordon visited the prisons; there he found dreadful dens of misery; over two hundred poor starving emaciated beings were confined therein; some bound with chains: some mere boys, some old men and women. Many of them were there simply on suspicion, and had never had a hearing. The cases were quickly and carefully enquired into, and before sunset that day, most of the unhappy wretches had their chains struck off and their freedom given them.

For many days, the markets and shops, and bazaars were finely illuminated; and the rejoicing for Gordon's presence and deeds was general and universal. Alas, however, the cloud which had so long hung over the Soudan began to thicken. The Madhi was not to be cheated of what he thought his rightful authority and dominion. The following letter recorded in Gordon's journal was received by him from the Madhi:—

> "In the name of God the merciful and compassionate;
> Praise be to God, the bountiful ruler, and blessing
> on our Lord Mahomet and peace. From the servant who
> trusts in God—Mahomet, the son of Abdallah.
>
> To Gordon Pasha of Khartoum,—May God guide him into the path of virtue, Amen! Know that your small steamer, named 'Abbas' which you sent with the intention of forwarding your news to Cairo, by the way of Dongola, the persons sent being your representative, Stewart Pasha, and the two Consuls, French and English, with other persons, has been captured by the will of God. Those who believed in us as the Madhi and surrendered, have been delivered; and those who did not have been destroyed. As your representative aforenamed, with the Consuls and the rest—whose souls God has condemned to the fire and to eternal misery: That steamer and all that was in it have fallen a prey to the Moslems, and we have taken knowledge of all the letters and telegrams which were in it, in Arabic and in Frankish (languages) and of the maps, which were opened to us (translated) by those on whom God has bestowed his gifts, and has enlightened their hearts with faith, and the benefits of willing submission. Also we have found therein the letters sent from you to the Mudir of Dongola, with the letters, &c., accompanying to be forwarded to Egypt and to European countries. All have been seized, and the contents are known. It should all have been returned to you, not being wanted here; but as it was originally sent from you, and is known to you, we prefer

to send you part of the contents, and mention the property therein, so that you may be certified: and in order that the truth may make a lasting impression on my mind—in the hope that God may guide thee to the faith of Islam, and to surrender to him and to us, that so you and they may obtain everlasting good and happiness. Now, first among the documents seized is the cipher dated September 22, 1884, 'to the Mudir of Dongola.' . . . On the back of which is your telegram to the Khedive of Egypt . . . We have also taken knowledge of your journal (daily record) of the provision in the granary . . . Also your letters written in European all about the size of Khartoum; and all about the arranging of the steamers, with the number of troops in them and their arms, and the cannon, and about the movements of the troops, and the defeat of your people, and your request for reinforcements, even if only a single regiment, and all about how your agent Cuzzi turned Moslem. Also many letters which had come to you from your lieutenants and what they contained of advice, also stating the number of Europeans at Khartoum . . . . Also the diary (registry) of the arms, ammunition, guns and soldiers . . . . We have also noted the telegrams of the officials and of the presidents of Courts, and of the Kadi and the Muftis, and Ulema, numbering 34, sent to the Mohurdâr of the Khedive in Egypt, dated Aug. 28th, 1884, in which they ask for succour from the Egyptian Government . . . Also your cipher telegrams to the Mohurdâr of the Khedive in which you explain that on your arrival at Khartoum the impossibility had become clear to you of withdrawing the troops and the employés, and sending them to Egypt, on account of the rebellions in the country, and on the closing of the roads; for which reason you ask for reinforcements which did not come . . . Also about your coming to Khartoum with seven men after the annihilation of Hicks' army; and your requesting a telegram to be sent to you in Arabic, in plain language, about the Soudan to show to the people of Khartoum—as the telegrams in European cipher do not explain enough . . . Also your letter to the Khedive of Egypt, without date, in which you ask to have English soldiers sent . . . And your letter to the President of the Council and the English Minister at Cairo, in which you speak of your appointing three steamers to go and inquire as to the state of Sennaar, and that you will send soldiers to Berber by the steamers to recapture it, sending with them Stewart and the Consuls, whom the Most High God has destroyed. Also we have seen the two seals engraved with our name to imitate our seals . . . . Tricks in making ciphers, and using so many languages, are of no avail. From the Most High God, to whom be praise, no secrets can be hidden. As to your expecting reinforcements, reliance for succour on others than God, that will bring you nothing but destruction, and cause you to fall into utmost danger in this world and the next. For God Most High has dispersed sedition through our manifestation, and has vanquished the wicked and obstinate people, and has guided those who have understanding in the way of righteousness. And there is no refuge but in God, and in obedience to His command, and that of His prophet and of His Madhi. No doubt you have heard what has happened to your brethren from whom you expected help, at Suakin and elsewhere, whom God has destroyed, and dispersed and abandoned. Notwithstanding all this, as we have arrived at a days journey from Omdurman and are coming please God, to your place, if you return to the most High God and become a Moslem and surrender to His Order and that of His prophet, and believe in us as the Madhi, send us a message from thee, and from those with thee, after laying down your arms and giving up the thought of fighting, so that I may send you one with safe conduct, by which you will obtain assurance of benefits of the blessings of this world and the next. Otherwise, and if you do not act thus, you will have to encounter war from God and His prophet. And know that the Most High God is mighty for thy destruction, as He has destroyed others before thee, who were much stronger than thee, and more numerous. And you, and your children and your property, will be for a prey to the monsters, and you will repent when repentance will not avail . . . And there is no succourer or strength but in God, and peace be upon those who have followed the Madhi. (*Guidance.*)

Postscript.—"In one of your cipher-telegrams sent to Bahkri and seized, you mention that the troops present in Bahr Gazelle and the Equator and elsewhere number 30,000 soldiers whom you cannot leave behind, even though you should die. And know that Bahr Gazelle and the Equator are both of them under our power and both have followed us as Madhi, and that they and their chiefs and all their officers are now among the auxiliaries of the Madhi. And they have joined our lieutenants in that part, and letters from them are constantly coming and going without hinderence or diminution of numbers. . . . By this thou wilt see and understand that it is not under thy command as thou thinkest. And for thy better information and our compassion for thee we have added this postscript.

(*Seal.*)

There is no God but Allah.
Mahomet is the prophet Allah.
Mahomet the Madhi, son of Abd Allah."

Year 1292.

Gordon's reply was just what we should expect from an officer of his temperament and experience. It is true things looked anything but cheering and our hero needed all his force of character and confidence in the God of Israel. This he had and kept brightly burning. To the Madhi he replied—

"Sheikh Mahomed Achmed has sent us a letter to inform us that Lupton Bey, Mudir of 'Bahr Gazelle' has surrendered to him, and that the small steamer in which was Stewart Pasha, has been captured by him, together with what was therein. But to me it is all one whether Lupton Bey has surrendered or has not surrendered. And whether he has captured twenty thousand steamers like the 'Abbas' or twenty thousand officers like Stuart Pasha or not; it is all one to me. I am here like iron, and hope to see the newly arrived English; and if Mahomed Achmed says that the English die, it is all the same to me. And you must take a copy of this and give it to the messenger from Slatin, and send him out early in the morning, that he may go to him. It is impossible for me to have any more words with Mahomed Achmed, only lead; and if Mahomed Achmed is willing to fight he had better, instead of going to Omdurman, go to the white hill by the moat."

(Signed) C. G. Gordon.

Gordon, though borne up by a sense of the Divine presence, yet he occasionally at least, felt as if he was leading a forlorn hope. We know not, nor can we ever know all the deeds of heroism he did for that down trodden people.

"A life long year unsuccoured and alone
He stemmed the fury of fanatic strife,
Till all lands claimed the hero as their own,
And wondering would he there lay down his life."

It is a mystery, and one that will never be solved, how he supported his vast family in Khartoum; for food had to be distributed to each individual member for months. It is also a sad but remarkable fact, that through the last ten months he had to depend upon the most unreliable and worthless of troops. And for four of those weary months, he had been without the cheering presence of his companion in arms, Colonel Stewart. Yet he held out bravely, courageously, and in hope of English help. At this juncture a poetess wrote—

"A message from one who went in haste
Came flashing across the sea,
It told not of weakness, but trust in God,
When it asked us—pray for me.
And since from Churches, and English homes,
In the day or the twilight dim,
A chorus of prayers went up to God—
Bless and take care of him:
A lonely man to those strange far lands,
He has gone with a word of peace;
And a million hearts are questioning
With a pain that cannot cease:

Is Gordon safe? Is there news of him?
What will the tidings be?
There is little to do but trust and wait;
Yet utterly safe is he.
Was he not safe when the Chinese shots,
Were flying about his head,
When trouble thickened with every day,
And he was sore bestead;
Was he not safe in his dreary rides,
Over the desert sands;
Safe with the Abyssinian King;
Safe with the robber bands;
We know not the dangers around him now,
But this we surely know—
He has with him in his hour of need,
His Protector of long ago;
He is not alone, but a Friend is by
Who answers to every need;
God is his refuge and strength at hand,
Gordon is safe indeed:
Safe in living, in dying safe, where is the need of pain;
We may pray—God give the hero long life,
But death would be infinite gain.

CHAPTER VIII

> "There is a better thing on earth than wealth, a better thing than life itself, and that is to have done something before you die, for which good men may honour you, and God your Father smile upon your work."
>
> —Geo. Macdonald.

The last Arab messenger that came from Khartoum before it fell, said, "Gordon goes every morning at sunrise to the top of his Palace wall, and with his large field glass, sweeps the horizon as far as possible, and notes as clearly as may be the position of the Madhi's forces, which now surrounded the City. As night falls, he visits the men at their various stations, to give them advice, or encouragement, as the case might be deemed necessary. In the daytime he studies his maps and reads his Bible, and a work on "Holy living," by Thomas à Kempis, and preserves such a faith in God as inspired all around him with a courage akin to his own.

> "He held the city, he so long
> Faithful mid falterers, mid much weakness strong,
> Upon those ramparts now he fought, he planned,
> That Citadel was by one true man well manned."

A letter from Kitchener reached Gordon, which raised his hopes and considerably brightened his prospects for the time being. It ran thus:—

> "Dear General Gordon.—Mr. Edgerton has asked me to send you the following:—'August 30th. Tell Gordon steamers are being passed over the Second Cataracts, and that we wish to be informed through Dongola exactly when he expects to be in difficulties as to provision and ammunition.' Message ends—"Lord Wolseley is coming out to command; the 35th regiment is now being sent from Halfa to Dongola. Sir E. Wood is at Halfa, General Earle, Dormer, Buller, and Freemantle are coming up the Nile with troops. I think an expedition will be sent across from here to Khartoum, while

another goes with steamers to Berber. A few words about what you wish to be done would be acceptable."

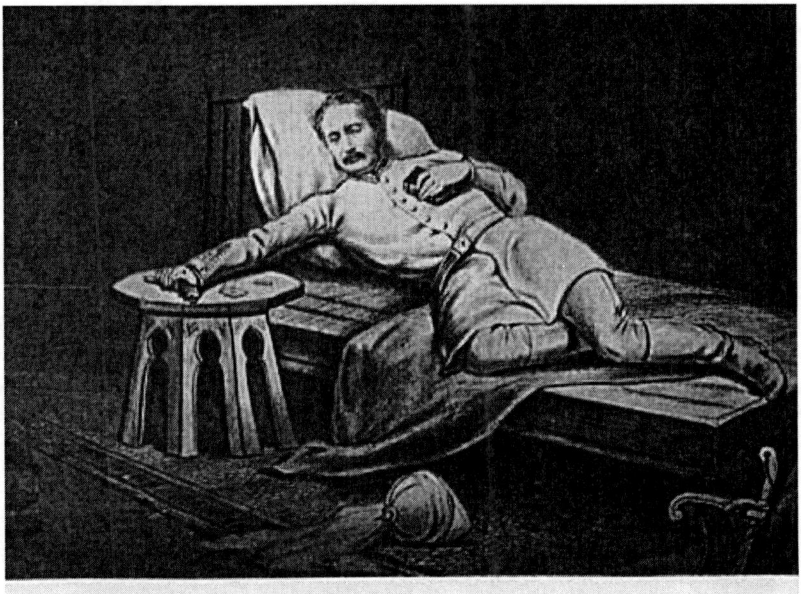

Gordon's Last Slumber.

In Gordon's journal he says:—"My view is this as to the operations of British forces. I will put three steamers each with two guns on them, and an armed force of infantry at the disposal of any British authority; will send these steamers to either Methemma opposite Shendy, or to the cataract below Berber to meet there any British force which may come across country to the Nile. . . . I cannot too much impress upon you that this expedition will not encounter any enemy worth the name in a European sense of the word; the struggle is with the climate and destitution of the country. It is one of time and patience, and of small parties of determined men backed by native allies, which are to be got by policy and money. . . . It is the country of the irregular, not of the regular. If you move in mass you will find no end of difficulties; whereas if you let detached parties dash out here and there, you will spread dismay in the Arab camps. The time to attack is the dawn, or rather before it, but sixty men would put the Arabs to flight just before dawn, while one thousand would not accomplish in daylight. The reason is that the strength of the Arabs is in their horsemen, who do not dare to act in the dark. I do hope that you will not drag on the artillery, it will only cause delay and do no good."

To his sister he writes:—

November 5th, 1884.

"Your kind letter, August 7th, came yesterday. We have the Madhi close to us, but the Arabs are very quiet. . . . . Terrible news—I hear the steamer I sent down with Stewart, Power, and Herbin (French Consul) has been captured and all are killed. I cannot understand it—whether an act of treachery by someone, or struck on a rock, it is to me unaccountable, for she was well armed and had a gun with her; if she is lost, so is the journal of events from Jan. 3rd, 1884, to Sept. 10th, 1884. A huge volume illustrated and full of interest. I have put my steamers at Metemma to wait for the troops. I am very well but very gray, with the continual strain upon my nerves. I have been putting the Sheikh-el-Islam and Cadi in prison; they were suspected of writing to the Madhi. I let them out yesterday. I am very grieved for the relatives of Stewart, Power, and Herbin."

Again he writes:—

Dec. 14th, 1884.

"This may be the last letter you will receive from me, for we are on our last legs, owing to the delay of the expedition. However, God rules all, and I know He will rule to His glory and our welfare. I fear that, owing to circumstances, my affairs pecuniarily are not over bright.

Your affectionate brother,
C. G. Gordon."

P.S.—"I am very happy, thank God, and, like Lawrence, 'I have tried to do my duty.'"

Meanwhile, Gordon is thus hemmed in. General Wolseley and his noble band are on their way to his relief. Many and peculiar are the difficulties of both climate, country, and foes; yet they face them like brave, true Englishmen. The journey from Cairo to Ambukol, a distance of more than one thousand miles, had been traversed without serious opposition. From here, however, as they near Khartoum, now about two hundred and fifty miles, taking the nearest desert route. Lord Wolseley seems here to halt and hesitate, whether it is best to go by the Nile, which, as shown on a map, takes a bend, forming the shape of a letter 'S' nearly; or whether to take the shortest cut and risk the opposition that may be expected. He eventually decides that the Camel Corps and a portion of the Infantry shall take the short cut; the desert route to Metemmeh: the rest to go by the Nile. It is evidently Wolseley's wish to punish the tribes who murdered Stewart, and his companions; so he orders the South Staffordshire, 38th, and the Royal Sussex, 35th, and the Black Watch, 42nd, to advance to Abu Hamed, which lies at the northern bend of the 'S,' which the Nile makes between Dongola and Metemmeh.

The Camel Corps are ordered to make a dash across the desert to the same place. Little did our force dream of the difficulties, dangers and deaths that lay before them as they entered upon that desert march. We only indicate some of them. On their march we are told that having nearly reached Abu Klea "we were turning into our zareba, when it was noticed that a group of some two hundred Arabs were on the hills, not far from us. Two shells were sent amongst them, which caused them to retire, but we soon found their sharpshooters had crept to within 1,200 yards of our right flank. Also they began to drop bullets into our midst, which were annoying and destructive. Half a company of Mounted Infantry were told off to drive them away. All officers were to see that the men were at their posts, with bayonets fixed, ready to jump to their feet at the very first alarm. With their overcoats on and their blankets wrapped around them, men lay down on that memorable night. All lights put out, all talking and smoking strictly prohibited. A deadly stillness, disturbed only by the whizzing or thud of the shot from the enemy's guns. Colonel Burnaby, who had managed somehow to find a place in the Expedition, expressed his great delight in having arrived in time to engage in what he now saw to be the prospect of a terrible struggle.

He stated, "that he had arrived at that time of life when the two things that interested him most were war and politics; and was just as happy in the desert fighting the Arabs, as he was at home slating an unworthy politician. Here, however, he was, and must face the conflict." January, 16th, 1885. About 10 p.m. The sentries came rushing into the lines. The officers called out, "stand to your arms men." The alarm, however, was false—only a feint on the part of the enemy. Still (says the writer), they kept harassing us by a continual dropping of shot from their long rangers. About 7.30 a.m., General Stewart prepared to send out an attacking column, with the object of driving them from the wells, which were now only four or five miles distant. The troops marched out—Mounted Infantry, Royal Artillery with three guns, Guards (this was the Front Face); Right Face—Guards, Royal Sussex; Left Face—Mounted Infantry, Heavy Cavalry Regiment. The 19th Hussars, under Colonel Barrow, numbering 90 sabres, were sent to left flank to advance along the spur of land on the north of the wady. Their duty was to move forward on a line paralleled with the Square, and prevent the enemy on our left from gaining the high ground across the little wady. A squadron of the 19th, thirty sabres strong, followed the Square, marching by the front right to assist the skirmishers. The Heavies were in charge of Colonel Talbot; the Guards by Colonel Boscowen; the Mounted Infantry by Major Barrow; the Naval Brigade by Lord Charles Beresford; the Royal Sussex by Major Sunderland; the Royal Artillery by Captain Norton; and the Royal Engineers by Major Dorwood. So they marched slowly forward. The progress was like that of some ponderous machine, slow, regular, compact, despite the hail of bullets that came from front, left and right, and ultimately from the rear. Some ten or twelve thousand Arabs it was seen had surrounded the Zareba. There was no retreat; it was "do or die!" About 9.50 a.m., about 5000 of the enemy were seen on the opposite side of the square, 400 or 500 yards distant, and seemed as if they would make a dash for our square. Dervishes on horseback, and some on foot, marshalled them, standing a few paces in front of the frantic host. With banners fluttering, tom-toms clamouring, and shouts of Allah, they began to move towards our square. The skirmisher's fire seemed to have no effect; though a few of them fell, they ultimately made a run towards us like the roll of a black surf. Lord Charles Beresford's superintendence was moved to the left face, rear corner, to be brought into action; for here they seemed to press the attack. Unhappily, before many rounds had been fired, the cartridges stuck and the weapon was useless. Still down came the Arab wave. One terrible rush of swordsmen and spearmen—scarcely any carrying guns—their rifle fire had practically ceased. In wild excitement, their white teeth glistening and the sheen of their brandished weapons flashing like thousands of mirrors; onward they came against us."

The writer says:—"A volley of shot was sent into them at 150 yards; at least one hundred Arabs fell, and their force wavered, as a man stops to get his breath; but the forces behind them came leaping over their falling brethren, and came charging straight into our ranks. I was at that instant inside the square, when I noticed our men shuffling backwards. Some say Colonel Burnaby issued an order for the men to fall back, but I did not hear it. Burnaby rode out apparently to assist our skirmishers, who were running in, hard pressed: all but one succeeding in getting inside the square: Burnaby went, sword in hand, on his borrowed nag, for his own had been shot under him that morning—he put himself in the way of a Sheik who was charging down on horseback. Ere the Arab closed with him a bullet from some in our ranks brought the Sheik headlong to the ground. The enemy's spearmen were close behind, and one of them clashed at Colonel Burnaby, pointing the long blade of his spear at his throat. Burnaby leant forward in his saddle and parried the Moslem's thrusts; but the length of the weapon (8 feet or more) made it difficult to deal a blow as desired. Once or twice the Colonel managed to touch him. This only made him the more alert. Burnaby fenced smartly, just as if he was playing in an assault-at-arms, and there was a smile on his features as he drove off the man's awkward points. With that lightning instinct which I have seen the desert warrior display in battle, whilst coming to another's aid, an Arab who had been pursuing a soldier, passed five paces to Burnaby's right and rear, and, turning with a sudden spring, this second Arab ran his spear point into the Colonel's right shoulder! It was but a slight wound, enough though to cause Burnaby to twist round in his saddle to defend himself from this unexpected attack. One of our soldiers saw the situation, and ran and drove his sword bayonet through this second assailant. As the soldier withdrew his steel the ferocious Arab wriggled round and tried to reach him. This he could not do, for he reeled and fell over. Brief as was Burnaby's glance at this second assailant, it was long enough for the first Arab to deliver his spear-point thrust full in the brave officer's throat. The blow brought Burnaby out of his saddle; but it required some seconds before he let go of the bridle-reins, and tumbled upon the ground. Half-a-dozen Arabs were now about him. With the blood gushing in streams from his gashed throat the dauntless Burnaby leaped to his feet, sword in hand, and slashed at the ferocious group. They were the wild shrieks of a proud man dying hard, and he was quickly overborne, and left helpless and dying! The heroic soldier who sprang to his rescue, was, I fear, also slain in the meleé, for though I watched for him, I never saw him get back to his place in the ranks.   But the square had been broken. The Arabs were driving their spears at our men's breasts. Happily, however, the enemy's ranks had been badly decimated by our bullets; yet they fought desperately, until bullet or bayonet stopped their career. Then from another quarter came a great onrush with spears poised and swords uplifted straight into our rear corner, the Arab horse struck like a tempest. The Heavies were thrown into confusion, for the enemy were right among them, killing and wounding with demoniacal fury. General Stewart himself rode into their midst to assist, but his horse was killed under him, and he was saved from the Arab spearmen with great difficulty: Lord Airlie received two slight spear wounds, and so did Lord C. Beresford. The Dervishes made terrible havoc for a few minutes. It was an awful scene, for many of the wounded and dying perished by the hands of the merciless Arabs, infuriated by their Sheiks, whose wild hoarse cries rent the air, whilst the black spearmen ran hither and thither thirsting for blood. Lord St. Vincent had a most providential escape. So great was the peril that the officers in the Guards and Mounted Infantry placed their men back to back to make one last effort to save the situation. "To me," says the writer, who was outside on the right face: "they appeared to spin round a large mound like a whirlpool of human beings."

Soon the enemy showed signs of wavering, for the fire of our English lads was fierce and withering. A young officer rallied a number of men on the rear; and these delivered a most telling fire into the enemy's ranks; the strained tension of the situation had been most severe, when at last the Arabs, two or three at first, then twenties and fifties, trotted off the field and in a very few minutes there was not an enemy to be seen. With cheer upon cheer, shouting until we were hoarse, we celebrated this dearly won victory. "Thus ended one of several terrible conflicts the men of the Expedition had to go through on their way to the beleaguered city." These lines of poetry, were written shortly after the news of this fierce engagement reached England:—

"They were gathered on the desert,
Like pebbles on the shore,
And they rushed upon the Christian
With a shout like cannon's roar;
Like the dashing of the torrent,
Like the sweeping of the storm,
Like the raging of the tempest,
Came down the dusky swarm.
From the scant and struggling brush-wood,
From the waste of burning sand,
Sped the warriors of the desert,
Like the locusts of the land:
They would crush the bold invader,
Who had dared to cross their path;
They were fighting for their prophet,
In the might of Islam's wrath,
They were savage in their fury,
They were lordly in their pride;
There was glory for the victor,
And heaven for him who died.
They were mustered close together,
That small devoted band;
They knew the strife that day would rage
In combat hand to hand.
And wild and weird the battle-cry
Was sounding through the air,
As the foe sprang from his ambush,
Like the tiger from his lair.

They knew the distant flashing
Of the bright Arabian spear,
As, spurring madly onward,
They saw the host appear
In numbers overwhelming,
In numbers ten to one;
They knew the conflict must be waged
Beneath the scorching sun;
They knew the British soldiers grave
Might lie beneath their feet;
But they never knew dishonour,
And they would not know defeat.
And swifter, ever swifter
Swept on the savage horde,
And from the serried British ranks
A murderous fire was poured;
And like the leaves in autumn
Fell Arab warriors slain,
And like the leaves in spring-time
They seemed to live again.
Midst the rattle of the bullets,
Midst the flashing of the steel,
They pressed to the encounter
With fierce fanatic zeal.
One moment swayed the phalanx,
One moment and no more;
Then British valour stemmed the tide,
As oft in days of yore.
At length the foe was vanquished,
And at length the field was won,
For the longest day had ended,
And the fiercest course was run.
Ye smiling plains of Albion!
Ye mountains of the north!
Now up and greet your heroes with
The honours they are worth.
Then pause and let a nation's tears
Fall gently on the sod
Where thy gallant sons are sleeping,
Whose souls are with their God."

Mr. Burleigh tells us that "History records no military events of a more stirring character, or situation more thrilling and dramatic than those through which Sir Herbert Stewart's flying column passed on this dreadful march. Through those terrible struggles with the followers of the Madhi, many a brave soldier fell and his body lies in the grave of the African desert. It did, however, seem as if through all the difficulties of the relieving forces, that Lord Wolseley would soon give the gallant defender of Khartoum succour and relief. The splendid victories won at Abu Klea Wells, and other places, and their march to join the Nile forces, clearly showed that they were terribly in earnest, and that they had the true British sympathetic heart.

Finding some of Gordon's steamers on the Nile, it was their first impulse to man them and force their way up to Khartoum at once. This was on January 21st, 1885. The General in Command learned that the steamers needed some repairs, and he (Sir Charles Wilson) deemed it necessary for the safety of his troops to make a reconnaissance down the river towards Berber before starting up to Khartoum. He took the steamers, which, though small as the Thames pleasure boats, had been made bullet-proof by the ingenuity and industry of the hero in distress; and with a small British force and two hundred and forty Soudanese (they also had in tow a nugger laden with dhura), they proceeded towards Berber some distance, and then, returning for their important work of relief, they pressed on to Khartoum in the face of the greatest dangers from the numerous fanatical Arabs, until they could see the city, and found to their horror and disappointment that Gordon's flag was torn down. The city had surrendered to the forces of the Madhi, and it could be seen to swarm with his followers! Treachery had been at work, as Gordon feared; and the brave defender of Khartoum sealed his fidelity with his own blood. We never doubted but he would "die at his post."

The Right Hon. W. E. Gladstone was on a visit to Holker Hall to see the Duke of Devonshire, when the sad tale was told of Gordon's betrayal and death. To add to the grief, the Queen, whose inmost soul had been stirred by the terrible news, sent to Mr. Gladstone and Lord Hartington a telegram couched in terms of anger and of blame, and this, not in cypher as was her wont, but plain and open.

Mr. Gladstone addressed to Her Majesty by return, in the most courteous manner possible, what may be considered a vindication of his actions in the matter and also that of his Cabinet:—

"To the Queen,—

> "Mr. Gladstone has had the honour this day to receive your Majesty's telegram, *en clair*, relating to the deplorable

intelligence received this day from Lord Wolseley, and stating that it is too fearful to consider that the fall of Khartoum might have been prevented and many precious lives saved by earlier action. Mr. Gladstone does not presume to estimate the means of judgment possessed by your Majesty, but so far as his information and recollection at the moment go, he is not altogether able to follow the conclusion which your Majesty has been pleased thus to announce. Mr. Gladstone is under the impression that Lord Wolseley's force might have been sufficiently advanced to save Khartoum, had not a large portion of it been detached by a circuitous route along the river, upon the express application of General Gordon, to occupy Berber on the way to the final destination. He speaks, however, with submission on a point of this kind. There is, indeed, in some quarters, a belief that the river route ought to have been chosen at an earlier period, and had the navigation of the Nile, in its upper region, been as well known as that of the Thames, this might have been a just ground of reproach. But when, on the first symptoms that the position of General Gordon in Khartoum was not secure, your Majesty's advisers at once sought from the most competent persons the best information they could obtain respecting the Nile route, the balance of testimony and authority was decidedly against it, and the idea of the Suakin and Berber route, with all its formidable difficulties, was entertained in preference; nor was it till a much later period that the weight of opinion and information warranted the definite choice of the Nile route. Your Majesty's Ministers were well aware that climate and distance were far more formidable than the sword of the enemy, and they deemed it right, while providing adequate military means, never to lose from view what might have proved to be the destruction of the gallant army in the Soudan. It is probable that abundant wrath and indignation will on this occasion be poured out upon them. Nor will they complain if so it should be; but a partial consolation may be found on reflecting that neither aggressive policy, nor military disaster, nor any gross error in the application of means to ends, has marked this series of difficult proceedings, which, indeed, have greatly redounded to the honour of your Majesty's forces of all ranks and arms. In these remarks, which Mr. Gladstone submits with his humble devotion, he has taken it for granted that Khartoum has fallen through the exhaustion of its means of defence. But your Majesty may observe from the telegram that this is uncertain. Both the correspondent's account and that of Major Wortley refer to the delivery of the town by treachery, a contingency which on some previous occasions General Gordon has treated as far from improbable; and which, if the notice existed, was likely to operate quite independently of the particular time at which a relieving force might arrive. The presence of the enemy in force would naturally suggest the occasion or perhaps even the apprehension of the approach of the British army. In pointing to these considerations, Mr. Gladstone is far from assuming that they are conclusive upon the whole case; in dealing with which the government has hardly ever at any of its stages been furnished sufficiently with those means of judgment which rational men usually require. It may be that, on a retrospect, many errors will appear to have been committed. There are many reproaches, from the most opposite quarters, to which it might be difficult to supply a conclusive answer. Among them, and perhaps amongst the most difficult, as far as Mr. Gladstone can judge, would be the reproach of those who might argue that our proper business was the protection of Egypt, that it never was in military danger from the Madhi, and that the most prudent course would have been to provide it with adequate frontier defences, and to assume no responsibility for the lands beyond the desert."

"Heroes have fought, and warriors bled,
For home, and love, and glory;
Your life and mine will soon be sped,
Then what will be the story?"

—J. Rushton.

The agonizing suspense in which our nation had been kept for weeks, was now at an end, and we learned the worst. The news fell like a thunderbolt upon our country! Within forty-eight hours of the time when Gordon would have heard the triumph ranting of English cheers, and once more clasped the faithful hands of British brother soldiers; treachery had done its worst. Thus ended this unique life's drama of one of the noblest hearts that ever beat in soldier's bosom, and one of the truest to his Queen, to his country, and to his God. The heart that had caused him to share his home with the homeless, and his bread with the hungry, that had led him to kneel in prayer by the dying; the heart that had so often throbbed for the misery of slavery, and the slave trade, as to risk his life as of no value to stop that cursed practice and traffic; that heart was pierced by the treacherous hands (in all probability) of the very man Gordon had made the greatest sacrifice to save. Such terrible news threw our land into universal mourning, and thousands wept for the hero that would never return.

The military correspondent of the "Daily News" at Dongola, writes: "Two men arrived here yesterday, April 11th, 1885, whose story throws some light on the capture of Khartoum. They were soldiers in Gordon's army, taken at the time and sold as slaves, but who ultimately escaped. Their names are Said Abdullah and Jacoob Mahomet. I will let them tell their own history." "After stating they were first taken at Omdurman, subsequently to the capture of Khartoum; were then stolen by arabs and sold to two Kabbabish merchants, and afterwards escaped from Aboudom to Debbah, from which place they had reached Dongola; they went on to relate the doings of Farig Pasha previously to the taking of Khartoum. I have given you some account of the story by telegraph, and it has been partly made familiar substantially through other channels. They continued: "That night Khartoum was delivered into the hands of the rebels. It fell through the treachery of the accursed Farig Pasha, the Circassian, who opened the gate. May he never reach Paradise! May Shaytan take possession of his soul! But it was Kismet. The gate was called Bouri'; it was on the Blue Nile. We were on guard near, but did not see what was going on. We were attacked and fought desperately at the gate. Twelve of our staff were killed, and twenty-two of us retreated to a high room, where we were taken prisoners, and now came the ending. The red Flag with the crescent was destined no more to wave over the Palace; nor would the strains of the hymns of His Excellency be heard any more at eventide in Khartoum. Blood was to flow in her streets, in her dwellings, in her very mosque, and on the Kenniseh of the Narsira. A cry arose, "To the Palace! to the Palace!" A wild and furious band rushed towards it, but they were resisted by the black troops, who fought desperately. They knew there was no mercy for them, and that even were their lives spared, they would be enslaved, and the state of the slave, the perpetual bondage with hard taskmasters, is worse than death. Slaves are not treated well, as you think; heavy chains are round their ankles and middle, and they are lashed for the least offence until blood flows. We had fought for the Christian Pasha and for the Turks, and we knew that we should receive no mercy. The house was set on fire: the fight raged and the slaughter continued till the streets were slippery with blood. The rebels rushed onward to the Palace. We saw a mass rolling to and fro, but did not see Gordon Pasha killed. He met his fate, we believe, as he was leaving the Palace, near the large tree which stands on the esplanade. The Palace is not a stone's throw, or at any rate a gun shot distance from the Austrian Consul's house. He was going in that direction, to the magazine on the Kenniseh, a long way off. We did not hear what became of his body, nor did we hear that his head was cut off; but we saw the head of the traitor Farig Pasha, who met with his deserts. We have heard it was the blacks that ran away; and that the Egyptian soldiers fought well; that is not true, they were craven. Had it not been for them, in spite of the treachery of many within the town, the Arabs would not have got in, for we watched the traitors. And now fearful scenes took place in every house and building, in the large Market Place, in the small bazaars; men were slain crying for mercy, but mercy was not in the hearts of those savage enemies. Women and children were robbed of their jewels of silver, of their bracelets, necklaces of precious stones, and carried off to be sold to the Bishareen merchants as slaves. Yes, and white women too, mother and daughter alike were carried off from their homes of comfort. Wives and children of Egyptian merchants, formerly rich, owning ships and mills; these were sold afterwards, some for 340 thaleries or more, some for 25, according to age and good looks. And the poor black women already slaves, and their children, 70 or 80 thaleries. Their husbands and masters were slain before their eyes . . . . this fighting and spilling of blood continued till noon, till the sun rode high in the sky. There was riot, wrangling, hubbub and cursing, till the hour of evening prayer. But the Muezzin was not called, neither were any prayers offered up at the Moslem Mosque on that dark day in the annals of Khartoum. Meanwhile the screeching devils bespattered with gore, swarming about in droves and bands, found very little plunder, so were disappointed, and sought out Farig Pasha, and found him with the Dervishes. 'Where is the hidden treasure?' they at once demanded of him. 'We know that you are acquainted with the hiding place. Where is the money and riches of the city and its merchants? We know that those who left Khartoum did not take away their valuables, and you know where it is hid.' The Dervishes seeing the tumult questioned him sharply, and addressed him thus: "The long expected one our Lord, desires to know where the English Pasha hid his wealth. We know he was very rich, and every day paid large sums of money; that has not been concealed from our Lord. Now therefore let us know that we may bear him word where all the money is hidden. Let him be bound in the inner chamber and examined; and the gates closed against the

Arabs." Farig was then questioned, but he "swore by Allah and by the souls of his fathers back to three generations, that Gordon had no money, and that he knew of no hidden treasure." "You lie (cried the Dervishes); you wish after a while to come and dig it out yourself. Listen to what we are going to say to you. We are sure you know where the money is hidden. We are not careful of your life, for you have betrayed the man whose salt you had eaten; you have been the servant of the infidel, and you have betrayed even him. Unless you unfold this secret of the buried treasure, you will surely die." Farig with proud bearing said, "I care not for your threats. I have told you the truth, Allah knows. There is no money, neither is there treasure. You are fools to suppose there is. I have done a great deed, I have delivered to your lord and master (the Madhi), the city which you never could have taken without my help. I tell you again there is no treasure, and you will rue the day if you kill me."

One of the Dervishes then stepped forward and struck him, bound as he was, in the mouth; then another rushed at him with his two-edged sword, struck him behind the neck so that with this one blow his head fell from his shoulders; (so perished the arch traitor); may his soul be afflicted! But as for Gordon Pasha the magnanimous, may his soul have peace!" The story of these men may, or may not be true, but it seems on the face of it trustworthy.

It is, however, out of harmony with the description given of Gordon's death by Slatin Pasha, who was taken a prisoner at the time of the fall of Khartoum, and had been kept for eleven years in captivity, but eventually made his escape. He was in attendance at the International Geographical Congress held at the Imperial Institute, and devoted to African affairs, when he told the story of his escape from Khartoum. He says "The City of Khartoum fell on the 16th Jan., 1885, and Gordon was killed on the highest step of the staircase of his Palace. His head was cut off and exhibited to Slatin whilst the latter was in chains, with expressions of derision and contempt."

We have no doubt now as to the fact that Gordon Pasha, the illustrious, the saintly, the brave defender, died doing his duty. In all civilized lands there are still men who tell of Gordon Pasha's unbounded benevolence; of his mighty faith, of his heroism and self-sacrifice, and they mourn with us the loss of one of the most saintly souls our world has ever known.

"Warrior of God, man's friend, not laid below,
But somewhere dead far in the waste Soudan,
Thou livest in all hearts, for all men know
This earth hath borne no simpler, nobler man."

Tennyson.

A most interesting and exquisitely touching letter was forwarded to the bereaved and stricken sister of our hero from the Khedive of Egypt, written from

"ABDUI PALACE,
"CAIRO,
"FEB. 24, 1885.

"Madam,—

"Altho' I do not wish to intrude upon the great sorrow which has fallen upon you in the death of your distinguished brother, the late General Gordon Pasha, yet as Egypt and myself have so much reason to deplore his loss, I desire to convey to you my heart-felt sympathy in the terrible bereavement it has been God's will you should suffer. I cannot find words to express to you the respect and admiration with which your brother's simple faith and heroic courage have inspired me: the whole world resounds with the name of the Englishman whose chivalrous nature afforded it for many years its brightest and most powerful example,—an example which I believe will influence thousands of persons for good through all time. To a man of Gordon's character the disappointment of hopes he deemed so near fruition, and the sudden manner of his death were of little importance. In his own words, he left weariness for perfect rest. Our mourning for him is true and real; as is also our loss, but we have a sure hope that a life and death such as his are not extinguished by what we call death. I beg to renew to you, Madam, the assurance of my sincere sympathy and respectful condolence.

"Mehemit Tewfik."

Also from the Queen, a letter full of womanly and queenly sympathy is here recorded from *The Daily News*:

"Dear Miss Gordon,—How shall I write to you, or how shall I attempt to express what I feel? To think of your dear, noble, heroic brother, who served his country and his Queen so truly, so heroically, with a self-sacrifice so edifying to the world, not having been rescued: that the promises of support were not fulfilled—which I so frequently and constantly pressed on those who asked him to go—is to me grief inexpressible: indeed it has made me ill. My heart bleeds for you, his sister, who have gone through so many anxieties on his account, and who loved the dear brother as he deserved to be. You are all so good and trustful, and have such strong faith, that you will be sustained even now, when real absolute evidence of your brother's death does not exist—but I fear there cannot be much doubt of it. Some day I hope to see you again to tell you all I cannot express. My daughter Beatrice, who has felt quite as I do, wishes me to express her deepest sympathy with you. I hear so many expressions of sorrow from abroad; from my eldest daughter The Crown Princess, and from my cousin the King of the Belgians—the very warmest. Would you express to your other sister, and your elder brother my true sympathy, and what I do so keenly feel, the stain left upon England for your dear brother's cruel, though heroic fate! Ever, dear Miss Gordon, yours sincerely and sympathizingly,

V.R.I."

A second letter from Her Majesty the Queen to acknowledge Miss Gordon's gift of her brother's Bible. The very Bible he used when with me in Manchester. His companion at Gravesend, and during his sojourn in the Soudan (first time). "It was so worn out (says Miss Gordon) that he gave it to me. Hearing that the Queen would like to see it, I forwarded it to Windsor Castle." And this Bible is now placed in an enamel and crystal case called "The St. George's Casket," where it now lies open on a white satin cushion, with a marble bust of General Gordon on a pedestal beside it.

Her Majesty writes:—

"Windsor Castle,
"March 16th, 1885.

"Dear Miss Gordon,—It is most kind and good of you to give me this precious Bible, and I only hope that you are not depriving yourself and family of such a treasure, if you have no other. May I ask you, during how many years your dear, heroic brother had it with him? I shall have a case made for it with an inscription, and place it in the library here, with your letter and the touching extract from his last to you. I have ordered, as you know, a Marble Bust of your Dear Brother to be placed in the corridor here, where so many busts and pictures of our greatest Generals, and Statesmen are, and hope that you will see it before it is finished, to give your opinion as to the likeness.—Believe me always yours very sincerely,

"Victoria R.I."

A most touching and I think true epitaph has been written in Greek and translated by Professor Jebb, of the University of Glasgow touching the death of General Gordon:—

> "Leaving a perpetual remembrance, thou art gone; in thy death thou wert even such as in thy life; wealth to the poor, hope to the desponding, support to the weak. Thou couldst meet desperate troubles with a spirit that knew not despair, and breathe might into the trembling. The Lord of China owes thee thanks for thy benefits; the throne of his ancient kingdom hath not been cast down. And where the Nile unites the divided strength of his streams, a city saw thee long-suffering. A multitude dwelt therein, but thine alone was the valour that guarded it through all that year, when by day and by night thou didst keep watch against the host of the Arabians, who went around it to devour it, with spears thirsting for blood. Thy death was not wrought by the God of war, but by the frailties of thy friends. For thy country and for all men God blessed the work of thy hand. Hail, stainless warrior! hail, thrice victorious hero! Thou livest and shalt teach aftertimes to reverence the council of the Everlasting Father."

Should he have been spared to return to our land—

"We had the laurels ready
That patient brow to crown,
But the traitors steel was swift and sharp
To strike our honours down.
God His own victor crowneth,
He counts not gain nor loss,
For the dauntless heart that battles
'Neath the shadow of the Cross.
Rest for the gallant soldier,
Where'er he lieth low,
His rest is still and deep to-day,
'Mid clash of friend and foe.
He stands amid the light he loved,
Whence all the clouds depart,

But there's a gap within our ranks,
And a void within our hearts."

Great men are usually measured by their character, not by their successes; but measured by either standard Gordon must be considered a *great* man. In him were incarnated all the highest characteristics of the heroes of our land, and other lands, and of the illustrious servants of God in all ages. His life was swayed by a noble purpose, and by this he was borne onward and upward in a career of noble doing and daring. He had courage of the very highest quality, and by this he carved his way into the very front rank of our heroes, and won remarkable distinctions in life's fiercest battles. His crowning characteristics were, I think, his genuineness, and unfailing trust in God. These, especially the latter, were the inspiration of his life; and these alone offer the truest explanation of his heroic deeds. Even in Spain his name had a fragrance that was attractive and beautiful. One of the papers *The El Dia*, of Madrid, wrote: "Where even the greatest events which occur abroad hardly attract the attention of the general public, the daring enterprises of General Gordon had excited the greatest interest. This was partly because of the immense importance of the drama which was being played in the Soudan, and because of the extraordinary development of the drama; but it was chiefly due to the sympathy of the people with the heroic champion of light and civilization; for his spotless honesty; for his valour, tried times without number; for his British tenacity; for his faith in his religion and country; for his keen insight; for his heroic unselfishness, and for all his other fine qualities. Gordon has become recognised in Spain as an original character, grand and complete, whom future generations will idealize, and whom history will call by the name of genius."

But Gordon, the great soldier and loveable Saint is dead; and he himself could wish no nobler ending of an unselfish life, after such a life of adventure, of heroism, and of humble trust in God.

A combination of strange, rare qualities helped to make him one of the most remarkable men our country has ever seen. As a Christian of rarest purity and consecration, and as a hero whose fame has filled two hemispheres, "His name shall be had in everlasting remembrance." He has added new chapters to the glorious stories of British pluck and heroism, and has left a name to which our young men will look back upon with pride; and the best of us will reverence, so long as truth, faith, self-devotion, and lofty sense of duty stir the admiration of men who are worthy to be called his fellow-countrymen. Our British nation thrills with a proud joy as it reflects upon the splendid achievements of that stainless life, now crowned with the laurels of martyrdom, and of an Empire's love.

The memorial in St. Paul's Cathedral most beautifully sets forth the leading traits in his character:—

> "Major General Charles George Gordon, C.B., who at all times and everywhere, gave his strength to the weak, his substance to the poor, his sympathy to the suffering, his heart to God.
>
> "Born at Woolwich, 28th Jan., 1838.
>
> "Slain at Khartoum, 26th Jan., 1885.
>
> "He saved an Empire by his warlike genius, he ruled vast provinces with justice, wisdom, power. And lastly, obedient to his Sovereign's command, he died in the heroic attempt to save men, women and children from imminent and deadly peril. 'Greater love hath no man than this, that a man lay down his life for his friends.'—St. John, xv. ch., v. 13.

THE MEMORIAL IN ST. PAUL'S CATHEDRAL.

"This monument is erected by his only surviving brother, whose eldest son also perished in the service of his country, as Midshipman in H.M.S. 'Captain,' and is commemorated with others in the adjoining recess."

"Gordon! thou lost ideal of our time,
While men believe not, and belief grows pale,
Before the daring doubters that assail;
We need thy child-like faith, thy gaze sublime,
That pierced the nearer gloom,
And still onward strode
Through death and darkness, seeing only God."

"Servant of Christ, well done,
Praise be thy new employ;
And while eternal ages run,
Rest in thy Saviour's joy."

Footnotes

[57] A work by the Rev. Wm. Arthur, which Gordon presented to me.

[63] The name of our Ragged School.